HOW NOT TO SHOOT FISH AND OTHER DEER THAT GOT AWAY

Edited by
CEDAR SANDERSON

How Not
To
Shoot Fish,
and
Other Deer
That
Got Away

Published by Sanderley Studios.

www.cedarwrites.com

Cover Art and Design, and Interior Illustrations by Cedar Sanderson

Edited by Cedar Sanderson

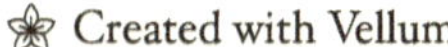 Created with Vellum

CONTENTS

FOREWORD

Dedication and Foreword

The genesis of this book really lies with Live! From the Blanket Fort, the podcast that evolved from the Old NFO and Lawdog's livestreams. The live comments on that particular 'cast are as lively as the hosts themselves, and the stories far-ranging. For a long time, the audience wanted to get a collection of hunting stories out of those two, and others. No, no... it can't be done, they said. Too short. Hunting stories tend to be short enough for comfortable telling around the campfire, embellished as time widens the gap between reality and the teller, but rarely longer than the shortest conventional story in publication.

My imagination started to kick into gear. I grew up in a family that hunted for the table, from a long line of hunters, trappers, and fishermen. You can find my Great-Grandad's stories in his memoir, *Confessions of a Poacher*, and I have the privilege of including a few of his in the second volume which will follow along soon. I also grew up reading everything and anything printed I could get my little paws on. Which included the various magazines like Field & Stream, Fur Fish Game, and others. I started to think about those, with their serialized stories, the hunting tales, and the wonderful pen-and-ink illustrations that enlivened the interior of those magazines in eras before color pages were the norm outside National Geographic.

This, coming on the tails of my having illustrated a short series of books in collaboration with Lawdog, gave me a bright idea. I'd do the hunting anthology. Only... I'd include a full-page illustration with each and every story. Sure, it was still likely to be short. But it would give good value, and it would hark back to beloved memories from my own childhood. I suspect the readers may share those memories, from similar sources.

To everyone's surprise, the response of authors to an invitation to tell their hunting tales was... well, it was humbling. They trust me to take care of their stories, and to that, I hope I have been up to the challenge. Enough tales came in to create two volumes of hunting stories, and I am delighted to present the first in these pages. The title is courtesy of Dorothy Grant, friend and fellow author, who humorously suggested it, and given how many hunting stories contain strong elements of humor, it suited the collection very well.

Remember, it's not about the ending, it's the adventure, when it comes to the hunt.

Cedar Sanderson
Editor, Illustrator
Somewhere in North Texas, September 2022

$\maltese$ I $\maltese$

Dove Season

By Lawdog

Some of my Gentle Readers may not realize how important
September 1 is.

It is the first day of Dove Season here in Texas, and for some,
a fairly important minor religious holiday.

So, there I was, wearing the (State-mandated) 144 square inches of
Daylight Orange on both chest and back, and the (State-mandated)
Daylight Orange headgear, tucked contentedly into a nook in a mesquite
tree-line.

In front of me, there was this lovely great patch of sunflowers --
crack cocaine to doves -- past that was a lake and behind me was not
only a tree-line, but was also east.

The plan was that the doves would wake up, fly out of the trees
towards the lake for a morning drink -- crossing my line of fire -- then,
thirst slaked -- would fly into the sunflower patch to break their fast --
again crossing my line of fire and affording me the opportunity to blow

the feathers off of the UN Symbol of Peace, prior to wrapping his little butt in bacon and searing him over a nice mesquite fire.

Now, since I am a County Employee, there is no way that I can afford a hunting lease. This limits my dove hunting opportunities to Public Land (see orange hunting requirements above), so I was fully cognizant that Reno and I would have a bit of company that morning.

When we had parked Reno's truck, there were no other vehicles anywhere, and I heard nothing as I waited for the sun to come up.

Just as the sun crested the horizon, I heard the double-click from Reno's radio, then the thump of his Mossberg 835 caused the first dove of the day to exclaim, "Holy [deleted], it's September 1 already?!" just before performing a classic Split-S and becoming a brown Mach 2 streak at grasstop level.

Unfortunately, this brought him right past my location, and I'm catching up to him with the brass bead of my 16 gauge when he pulls a batwing turn that should have been impossible without a G-suit ...

... and I hear this voice on the far side of the dove yell, "Jeff, Jeff, Jeff -- izzat a dove?!"

"Oh," sayeth that little voice in the back of my head, "bugger."

"Shootshootshoot!" shrieks the heretofore unseen Jeff.

I hit the dirt, finding myself nose-to-nose with a spider who -- obviously a veteran of previous dove hunts -- had all eight legs covering his head.

Foomfoomfoomfoomfoom!

When the shooting died down, I cautiously peered over my comforting tree root as a cattle egret who had been circling overhead -- smugly confident in his neutral status -- dirt-darted into the ground about twenty feet away.

"Jeff, Jeff! I got his butt, Jeff!"

Down above the sunflower patch, the absolutely untouched dove snap-rolled and cut in the afterburner just above the tops of the flowers, leaving -- I swear to God -- petals tossing in his wake -- as the world exploded.

There wasn't that much ground-to-air fire above Baghdad.

Either time.

The dove went feet-wet over the lake and disappeared in the early-morning fog to the accompaniment of the ***Top Gun*** theme.

I spit out some grass, looked sideways at the spider and commented, apropos of nothing: "Sounds like the magazine plug law is more like a magazine plug suggestion around here." The spider cocked a snook in my general direction and hurried off to the local air-raid bunker.

My radio crackled, Reno warbling: "It's raining lead ... Hallelujah! It's raining lead ... Amen!"

I hauled myself to my feet, checked my Remington Model 11, and wandered off to check my buddy. As I walked up, he cocked an eyebrow at me, took off his State-approved Daylight Orange ball cap and brushed 7 1/2 shot off of it.

"Didn't we find a rule that says you've got to wear a certain amount of orange if you're hunting on public land?"

I nod.

"Of the three thousand [deleted] hunters out here, how many orange vests d'you see?"

"Yours and mine." I pause meditatively. "How many of those auto-chuckers have magazine plugs, you think?"

He snorts, "Yours."

Long pause, as the gentle patter of falling 7 1/2 shots rustled around us.

"I'll bet the catfish are biting out at Kickapoo."

"You read my mind."

So we took Reno's wife and daughter out to the lake and caught fish on the opening day of Dove Season.

❧   2   ❧

Winter Wings

By Kelly Grayson

The alarm rudely drags me back to wakefulness. 4:00 am comes all too quickly, even when you're looking forward to getting up. Quietly, I slip out of bed and pad across the room to turn it off. A lump stirs under the covers, and the comforter slips back to reveal a black head, one eye opened balefully. She doesn't lift her head from the pillow.

"Time to get up, soup hound," I yawn. "It's a new day."

Sprite's tail thumps twice under the comforter, and she raises her head for a moment, regarding me. She yawns and licks her chops, and then, as if the effort has totally sapped her strength, lets her head fall back to the pillow, as limp as a rag doll.

Behold the world-class, championship retriever. Exquisitely bred, painstakingly trained to be a duck fetcher without peer... who apparently believes her mission in life is to hold down the bed and guard the couch.

Chuckling quietly, I quickly get dressed. Polypropylene thermal underwear, camo shirt, neoprene sock liners, wool socks. Synthetic fleece wader pants, the kind with the stirrups, complete the ensemble. There are few things more uncomfortable than standing in freezing water with one pant leg bunched up at knee level underneath your waders.

Except of course, a leak in the waders at crotch level. That always ranks high in Misery Quotient.

Through it all, Sprite lays on the pillow like a dead thing, refusing to relinquish the warmth of the bed for a cold floor. She's a lot like a soldier; both know that they'll get plenty of personal discomfort and misery on the job, so they might as well take advantage of creature comforts while they're available. There is no need to practice being wet and cold. It comes naturally.

It's the call lanyard that finally does it. The musical tinkle of duck bands as I slip the lanyard over my head transforms sixty pounds of inert bed warmer into a whirling dervish of nervous energy. She knows what that sound means.

Sprite bounds from the bed and makes a beeline for the back door. She spins a tight circle around my pile of gear sitting at the door and bounces excitedly on her front feet, her eyes shining in the dark. She whines softly.

If I didn't know better, I'd say the little bitch is giggling.

"Go do your business," I tell her, opening the door into the exercise yard. Instantly, Sprite bolts through the gap, and bedlam ensues. Twenty dogs all start yammering at once. I turn on the yard lights, slip on a pair of camp shoes and step outside, barking *"QUIET!"*

One reminder is usually all it takes, but the silence won't last long with Sprite running around loose. She prances around saucily, sniffing this, investigating that, flaunting her freedom in a canine *neener neener neener* at the poor mutts that have to stay behind.

While she's busy reminding the other dogs of her favored place in the pecking order, I quickly turn on the water and wash down the kennels, the hose stiff and unyielding in the cold. Occasionally, the braver dogs venture outside to bark, but a stream of near-freezing water from a one-inch hose is all it takes to send them scrambling back to the warmth of their houses.

By the time I've rolled and drained the hose, Sprite is waiting expectantly for me at the back door. She *whuffs* softly, the condensation from her breath rising like smoke signals over her head. It's cold out here.

She waits impatiently for me to open the door, looking at me as if to say, "Hey, *you're* the one with the opposable thumbs. I can't be expected to do *all* the work around here."

Inside, she paces nervously as I fill my thermos with hot water from the coffeemaker. I'm not much of coffee drinker, but hot chocolate on a frigid morning is always nice. It's even better when you're watching a sunrise over the steam wafting from your cup.

As Sprite nervously paces the office that doubles as a studio apartment, I quickly check my gear bag before heading outside. Every few circuits, she'll stop at the door and whine softly.

Yes Sprite, I know I packed it last night. Yes, I am that anal. Do I rush you when you're doing important dog business, like sniffing the ass of a stranger or licking yourself? No, I let you be a dog. You can return the favor my ignoring my OCD.

Besides, this is more than just a bag filled with miscellaneous duck hunting detritus. There are three generations of tradition in that bag. A side pocket holds my Granddaddy's hand warmers, the old-fashioned kind that use lighter fluid instead of those wimpy fuel sticks. On the opposite side, you'll find my Daddy's favorite call. A small wood call with a brass reed, it takes a lot of skill to blow, but nothing sounds sweeter in the flooded timber. I never use it, yet I take it with me on every trip as a talisman of simpler times. I think the hunting gods would approve.

In the center compartment you'll find my gloves and shells – two boxes of standard steel #4, plus a box of 3-inch magnum steel #2 for my hunting partners. I love my buddies, but some of them couldn't hit a bull in the ass with a bass fiddle, and they seem to think that more and bigger pellets will make up for a poor swing. They're forever running low on shells.

The bag itself was a gift from my brother, given one Christmas years ago when I was finally old enough to go hunting on my own. The original camouflage pattern has long since faded into a mosaic of mud from hunts past, each stain a memory, every blemish with its own story to tell. There's red clay from the Katy prairie in Texas, black mud from the

Louisiana marsh, bark stains from pin oaks in the Arkansas river bottoms.

Tucked in an interior pocket are my Gerber multi-tool, a roll of decoy line, several steel tree- climbing steps, and my GPS receiver. Filling in the empty spaces are an aspirin bottle holding extra duck call reeds, another holding strike-anywhere matches, a styptic pencil, extra decoy weights, a folding limb saw, and enough honey buns and candy bars to fuel a battalion of kindergartners.

Sounds like a lot of stuff, doesn't it? It is, and every one of my hunting partners carries one much like it. Don't try to understand it. A duck hunter's blind bag is the male equivalent of a woman's purse. Just be thankful I gave you a peek into the mystery of mine.

Satisfied that I indeed had packed all that I needed, I sling my blind bag across my shoulder, grab my Remington 870 and my wader bag, and head outside into the cold. Sprite leads the way to the gate in the privacy fence and prances nervously, nose pressing urgently against the gate as I fumble with the latch.

My shoes crunch across the frozen ground, and a rime of frost sparkles like diamonds on my decoy bags in the boat. The air is clear, the stars like pinholes in the blanket of night. The temperature is hovering just below freezing, and there's a stiff north breeze hinting at the arctic front headed our way.

Clear and getting colder, with a north wind. Perfect.

I WEDGE MY WADERS ON THE PASSENGER FLOORBOARD BELOW THE heater vents, and I park Sprite atop them just in case. I *hate* putting on cold waders.

I start the truck engine and let it warm up while I stow my gear. My blind bag and shotgun go in the compartment under the boat seat. On-board battery charger gets unplugged, seats folded down, and I make a cursory check for anything not tied down. A quick check of the plugs, hitch lock and trailer lights, and we're on the road. By the time we hit the highway, Sprite has managed to inch across the seat until her head rests on my thigh.

Normally I'd pick the guys up and we'd stop for breakfast at Ray's

PeGe, maybe spend a half hour eating runny eggs and swapping hunting lies. There's no time for it this morning, however. Six weeks into the duck season, and the Ouachita River is finally high enough to flood the northern end of the refuge. Every hunter and his brother-in-law will be jockeying for a hunting spot.

I roll into the parking lot at a quarter till five, gratified to see that I am the first one there. Even during midweek in December, by daybreak the lot will be full of four-wheel-drive trucks towing boat trailers. In Louisiana, duck hunting is a religion, and the most devout of us worship early and often. It's always nice, though, when you get to be the first worshipper at the communion rail.

The cold hits me with a jolting slap as I open the truck door. Before I can get it open fully, Sprite scrambles across my lap and bolts for the picnic area, nosing around the grass, the tables, snuffling at the water's edge.

Getting wound up, I smile inwardly. *Just like always.*

Something splashes out there in the river, and Sprite's muscles tense, warning me just in time.

"*No. Here,*" I command quietly, just loud enough to be heard. She doesn't like it, but she backs away from the water and comes to sulk at my side. I suppress a smile as I go about the business of readying my boat for launch. I have no intention of sitting with a wet retriever in my lap for half an hour waiting for Paul to arrive.

And Paul is *always* late to arrive.

The stern tie-downs are stiff, the straps coated in frost and the buckles frozen, but eventually they yield, under protest, to repeated kicks from my size 12 boot. Sprite follows me around as I check the drain plugs again, check my running lights and battery, check to make sure the bow line is attached, and slowly back the trailer into the water. When I get back out of the truck to beach my boat, she elects to stay inside, parked comfortably under the heater vent.

See? Soup hound.

As I sit in the warmth of my truck, Sprite's head resting in my lap, I allow myself to doze fitfully, awakened every few minutes by the glow of headlights on my eyelids as a steady procession of hunters arrive and launch their boats. Sprite doesn't stir, unless you count the insistent prod of her nose if I fail to stop scratching the sweet spot behind her right ear.

Finally, a glow of headlights is accompanied by a familiar growl of custom truck exhaust, and Sprite lifts her head from my lap expectantly. Paul's Chevy noses into the parking spot next to mine, and he grins wickedly as he rolls down his window.

"Pardon me," he smirks. "Would you happen to have any Grey Poupon?"

I answer with a pointed glance at my watch, and a one-fingered salute.

"Forgot my waders," he apologizes half-heartedly. "Had to go back and get 'em." Paul has offered a variation of this excuse every day we've hunted for the past fifteen years. He doesn't even try to sell it. It doesn't have to be a believable excuse. He just has to offer one.

"Maybe you should just set your alarm clock thirty minutes ahead," I retort with my part of the ritual. I'm not really pissed. I just have to pretend to be. That's my part of the arrangement.

"So what's the plan?" he asks as we transfer his gear to the boat.

"Well, Plan A was to set up in the north corner of the bean field," I chide, "but that was before twelve damned boats launched ahead of us. By the time we get set up, we'll probably be able to walk across the bean field on all the decoys. So, I guess we try Plan B."

"Which is...*what*, exactly?" he asks impatiently.

"Drive north until we don't hear any other boat motors," I shrug. "Then we'll turn into the woods and keep going until the prop starts hitting bottom, or until we don't see spotlights any more. Whichever comes first."

"Sounds good to me," Paul replies. "Do I get to work the dog this time?"

"Nope."

"Why not?" he asks petulantly as I climb into the boat.

"Because," I explain, for the hundredth time, "you have to be smarter than the dog, Paul. She runs all over you. Besides, you're a bad influence. You feed her Vienna sausages and peanut butter crackers, and at night her farts peel the paint off the walls."

"Your Daddy is a spoilsport," he pouts, kneeling down next to Sprite and making kissing noises until she licks his face. "Your Daddy *mistreats* you, and takes *all* the credit for what a good dog you are, yes he does! Your Daddy exploits your talents for his own financial gain, yes he does! But Sprite *loves* her Uncle Paul, doesn't she? Yes her does, and her Uncle Paul loves *her*."

"When you're through sucking up to the dog, Uncle Paul," I suggest wryly, "how about untying the boat and pushing us away from the bank?"

Sprite jumps aboard and Paul pushes us out into the current. I lower the motor, prime the fuel bulb, and yank the starter rope.

Nothing.

"Don't do this to me now, you whore," I mutter under my breath. I engage the choke and yank the starter rope again, and the motor replies with a dull, flat cough, *"Whut."*

"You leave me drifting in the $&&^# current, I swear I'll drop your worthless butt in the river and buy myself a new Evinrude."* Savagely, I yank the starter rope again.

"Whut...whut...WHUT...WHUT...whutwhutwhutwhutwhutwhut...wh..."

"You %$&# heartless tease,"* I fume quietly. *"You did that on purpose."* I turn off the choke, count slowly to ten, and once again pull the starter rope.

"Whutwhutwhutwhutwhutwhut..." the motor purrs agreeably. Relieved, I gingerly open the throttle, steering us into the channel and pointing us north. As I open the throttle fully, the motor abruptly dies. The ultimate act of defiance.

"You black-hearted bitch, worthless son-of-a whore!" I scream in apoplectic fury. *"That's it! I get us back to the bank, and I'm selling your ass! Worthless piece of crap!"*

"Starter fluid," Paul suggests helpfully from his warm nest at the front of the boat. "Spray some in the air intake."

Starter fluid? STARTER FLUID???

Philistine.

Obviously, the man knows nothing about cold-natured Mercury outboard motors. Anyone who knows anything about outboards knows that uncontaminated fuel, judicious use of the choke, and liberal amounts of profanity are the generally accepted methods for starting a Mercury motor. Starter fluid is nothing more than crack for outboard motors. It revs 'em up for a little bit, but they get hooked on it, and pretty soon nothing else works, even when they're warm. Then I'd still have a contrary motor, with a crack habit.

Gritting my teeth, I stand up in the back of the boat, brace one foot on the motor, and yank the starter cord one last time. This time, the old girl starts immediately, and responds with a deep- throated roar when I open the throttle. Grinning, I steer us into the middle and head upriver at full throttle, navigating by moonlight.

I love you too, baby. I just wish you wouldn't make me cuss you every morning.

I AM BRACED BY THE RIDE UPRIVER, INTO THE TEETH OF A COLD NORTH wind. Paul and Sprite lay huddled in the front of the boat, seeking to stay out of the wind, while I turn my cap around backwards and grin into the wind, the tears streaming from the corners of my eyes and marching back into my hair. This feeling is what I live for.

Soon enough, I begin to overtake the boats that launched while I was cursing my motor, and even half a dozen that launched well before I did. All of them are motoring at a snail's pace, spotlights vainly trying to pierce the fog, cautiously trying to navigate the channel, desperately seeking the fluorescent ribbons or reflective buttons they've carefully hung to mark the way to their favorite hunting places. One is slowly creeping up Mud Lake, unaware that he has left the main channel. He'll run aground soon.

I blow past them all, my path lit by nothing more than the dull green and red glow of my bow light, illuminating little more than a boat length of the river in front of us.

That's more than enough.

This river is where I belong. Over the years I've come to know it well, just as well as the path to the bathroom in my own home. Every curve, every bend and channel buoy, I can see them in my mind's eye well before they loom like specters out of the mist. It's like exploring the curves of a familiar lover; you don't need the lights on to enjoy each other.

The landmarks fly by as I wind my way upstream. The old barge pilings off the East bank, right there in the first bend, loom like rotten teeth in a gaping mouth. The bluffs that mark the route to the prairie potholes, the entrance to Frank LaPierre Creek, the tiny gap in the bank that everyone ignores, that few people know leads to a beautiful cypress lake nestled right against the levee. The pipeline crossing that leads to the bean field only has half a dozen boats on it, their spotlights crossing the sky like a Hollywood premiere.

I'm briefly tempted to try the bean field. I know the sweet spots, the ones often overlooked by everyone else. I could get in the before most of the others, set up my rig and shoo people away until dawn. We'd kill ducks there, I'm sure.

But this is about more than just killing ducks. There are too many people here. Even if I am the first to set up, the latecomers will crowd in anyway. The ducks love the area, and for that reason, so do all the hunters. I spoke before of duck hunting as a religion in Louisiana. In places like the bean field, or the lakes branching off Frank LaPierre Creek, you will not want for fellow congregants.

I prefer to do my worship in a quiet cathedral of pin oaks, with little company save for a close friend and my dog. Occasionally, I meet a stranger in these cathedrals, and we acknowledge each other with a quiet word and a knowing smile, and move off to a respectful distance. We both know how hard it is to get back in here, and how precious the solitude we both seek.

A familiar bend in the river looms ahead, and I cut the throttle a bit, scanning the left bank for the channel buoy and the houseboat moored a hundred yards north of it. I ease up alongside the houseboat and cut the motor, and Paul stirs and raises his head.

"We there already?" he yawns, stretching. Sprite stands on the deck at the front of the boat, tail wagging.

"Not yet," I reply quietly. "Grab hold of the railing there and hold us in place for a bit."

I turn and look behind us. The spotlights are gone, lost in countless bends of the river twenty miles behind us. The only sound is the gurgle of the current rushing past us. We've been motoring for close to an hour, and my hands are stiff. I pull off my gloves and check my watch.

Five minutes till six. We'd better hurry.

"Push us off," I order. "We've got thirty five minutes to find a spot and set up."

"Set up *where?*" Paul wonders. "All I see are a bunch of damn trees!"

"Just sit in the front of the boat and watch for limbs," I smile knowingly. "We'll find something."

Dubiously, he perches in the front of the boat, Indian style. "Crazy bastard gonna get us lost up here," I can hear him grumble. "Prob'ly in Arkansas by now, and I don't even have an Arkansas license..."

Chuckling to myself, I turn at a right angle to the channel and motor west, directly into the woods. It doesn't take long before the branches start to slap at Paul, threatening to knock him out of the boat.

"Hey, dammit!" he gripes. "Slow down a little! Let's at least turn on a light so we can see where we're going!"

"Lie down on the front deck, Paul," I order. "Grab the spotlight, but only turn it on very briefly. Shine on the water right in front of the boat and keep a sharp eye out."

"For *what?*"

"Stumps, and rafts of pin oak acorns," I grin. "I don't need the light to navigate."

"We don't need to find an open spot?" he asks dubiously, turning to look at me and blinding me with the spotlight in the process.

"Nope. Now please get the light out of my eyes and look for stumps."

Grumbling under his breath, Paul lies on his belly on the front deck, chin propped on the bow light, spotlight flickering occasionally on the water in front of the boat. Frequently he calls out course corrections and warnings. "Come right... now straight ahead... ease to the left... duck your head, big limb coming down the right side... it would be helpful if I knew where the hell we were going..."

I'd tell you, but I don't know myself. Where we're going isn't so much a place as a feeling. I'll know it when we get there. It'll feel right.

Twenty minutes pass, and innumerable logs and stumps, and I estimate we're perhaps a mile off the river channel. I cut the motor, and plumb the water at the stern of the boat with a short paddle.

Hip deep. Almost right.

"This is it," I announce. Let's tie up the boat and unload our gear."

Paul gingerly climbs out of the bow, and promptly snags his foot on a log, almost falling in. He drops to his knees, and the water comes to within an inch of the top of his waders. "Uhhh, a little help please?" he begs.

"It's not a duck hunt until you do a hat-floater," I observe wryly, walking over and helping him to his feet. "You falling in is always a good omen."

"Screw you," he retorts, once he is sure of his footing. "And I'm not always falling in."

"You could put an inch of water in the Wal Mart parking lot..." I recite.

"... and Paul would find a way to fall in over his head," he finishes snidely as he straps a decoy bag across his shoulders. "You know, that was funny only the first few hundred times y'all said it."

"Nonsense," I chuckle as I spread camo netting across the boat. "It's funny *every* time, because it's true."

"Only one sack of decoys?" Paul asks, nodding at the other sacks still in the boat. "And what am I, the pack mule?"

"Yep," I retort, "and I'm the guide. Let's go, Sprite." I grab her dog stand, my blind bag and gun, and wade further into the woods. I go slowly, pushing my feet along the bottom carefully, making little more than a ripple as I feel for obstacles. Behind me, Paul sounds like an epileptic having a seizure in the bathtub. Sprite swims ahead of us, meandering through the trees aimlessly. Occasionally, she swims back and makes circles around me, whining softly.

Almost there, soup hound. You can rest in a minute.

After a couple hundred yards, the water is only up to our thighs, and my flashlight illuminates the occasional raft of acorns piled against a floating log.

This is the place. This feels right.

"Let's set up right here," I announce. "I'll take this big pin oak, and you take that one on the right. Throw out a dozen or so decoys and stash the rest somewhere."

In just a few minutes, the thunder of distant guns will announce legal shooting hours, even though the vague pinkening of the eastern skies announce that actual sunrise is still thirty minutes away. Paul rushes to set out the decoys, and true to character, he throws them out haphazardly, with no regard to spacing. As long as they're upright, he couldn't care less about anything else.

True to *my* character, I am overly picky about my decoy spread, so I go behind him and rearrange them, spreading them out, segregating them, moving most of the spread upwind of us, leaving a big open pocket right in front of us. I place a hen decoy on the downwind side of the pocket, and three wood duck decoys in a cluster on the far edge, forty yards out. Perfect range markers. When I'm done, I take a few seconds to admire my masterpiece.

Perfect. When the ducks make their downwind swing, they'll still be able to see the lone hen out there. They'll make their upwind landing pass, right up the chute to the pocket right in front of us. Perfect.

That is, if the ducks cooperate. When I was a boy, I eagerly devoured the pages of *Outdoor Life* or *Field and Stream*, scrupulously memorizing the decoy patterns occasionally illustrated there. The Modified J, The Fishhook, The Funnel...I knew them all. Skillful calling and a little trickery will often lure them close enough for a shot, but I fear the nuances in decoy arrangement matter to no one but me.

That's not the point, though. *I* like the way it looks. If the ducks don't like it, I'll rearrange them into another pattern that will be *just* as perfect, because *that's* the pattern that will pull thousands of greenheads from the sky into this little pothole. Or the next pattern will. Favored decoy spreads are as unique and personal a thing as say, blind bags or your relationship with your outboard motor.

I strap Sprite's dog stand to my tree, help her climb aboard, and screw a couple of tree steps into the trunk off to one side. I hang my 870 from one, and my blind bag and thermos from the other. Paul watches the whole operation with a pitiful expression on his face, standing there with his blind bag still hanging from his shoulder.

"Here, ya' big baby," I relent, wading over and handing him my last tree step. When you're standing in thigh-deep water, you don't *toss* anything that doesn't float.

"Thanks," Paul grins. "Just for that, I'll try not to outshoot you this morning,"

"You couldn't hit water if you fell out of the boat," I retort. Both of us know I'm the better wing shooter, but not by much. With a rifle, I can't match him. But Paul is just that – a *shooter*. Hunting is secondary to him. He'd have been just as happy fighting the crowd at the bean field, content in the knowledge that he could scratch down more ducks than anybody else.

I settle in at my tree and check my watch, and Sprite shivers and whines softly. Ice is already forming on her coat.

Six thirty-two. Three minutes until legal shooting time.

To the east, distant guns thunder over the rice fields.

"The mudpuppies are starting a bit early, ain't they?" Paul winks, thumbing shells into his gun. "Shoot the Hollywoods first?"

"Or gadwalls, or teal. Maybe even widgeon," I agree. "Whatever presents itself. The mallards will be along later." In the flooded timber, wood ducks are the first to stir, rocketing through the trees like agile little missiles, announcing their passing with a screech and a piercing squeal. They're among the flashiest of ducks, colorful and gaudy, and more than just a little flighty. Hence the nickname, *Hollywood Mallards*.

South of here, there is a cypress brake that winds its way through the pin oak flats, and the Hollywoods flock to it like starlets to a nightclub opening. They weave through the trees at blistering speed, wave after wave of them until the sun finally climbs above the horizon. Hunting that brake is a non-stop, can't-keep-your-gun-loaded, barrel-melting, kamikaze storm of crazy little ducks with green heads and bright red eyes. You don't even need a call or decoys. After the dawn flight, the wood ducks evaporate into thin air and the place is barren.

"Hollywoods out front," Paul hisses, nodding downwind. A distant screech gets steadily louder, and I pick up three blurs moving through the trees, barely visible in the dim light. I barely have time to reach for my gun before they flash over us...

Eeeeeeeek... eeeeeeeek... eeeeeeeek... BOOM. BOOM.

Paul's sweet sixteen barks twice, and two drakes crumple in midair. I swing on the third, and... *click.*

Damn. I knew I forgot something.

"You know, I think it works better if you actually *load* your gun," Paul observes innocently.

I give him the finger, and look at Sprite. She's focused on something behind our tree, leaning over the edge of her platform, rump hovering just off the seat. Every muscle is corded and trembling. "*Sprite,*" I command quietly. With this dog, it's not so much a command as a release. A *command* would be required to stop her. By the time the sibilant *S* has passed my lips, she has launched herself in a smooth, graceful leap. Swimming powerfully, she is on the duck in seconds, and turns back to me.

I help her back onto the platform, take the duck from her, and see that she is locked in again. This time, when I give her release, she lets out a jubilant little yip as the launches herself off the platform. I toss Paul's duck to him and load my gun as she swims for the second bird.

"Nice shooting," I say.

Paul grins and starts to say something, then freezes and lowers his head. I know that look.

I lean back against the trunk of my tree and roll my shoulders around, scanning the sky behind me. I search desperately for the birds Paul has spotted, and see nothing until...

... there, below the tree tops, feet down and committed. Four of them. Widgeon.

Time slows down as I point at the highest bird, barely ten feet off the water, just hanging there in space, right beyond the bead at the end of my barrel. My gun recoils once, and the bird folds in a slow-motion puff of feathers. Without conscious thought, my barrel picks up one of his compatriots, rising from the water, wings clawing for altitude. My gun barks again and I see him stagger in midair, wings still pumping furiously. The clack of the slide is as loud to my ears as the shot, and the barrel is just a half-noticed shadow as the drake climbs above the trees, my barrel swinging beyond his head now as my 870 bucks for a third time. The only thing vividly in focus is that drake widgeon, silhouetted against the brightening sky as my third shot hits him and he locks his wings and sails...

... and just like that, time starts spinning again as he splashes down in a shower of twigs, perhaps a hundred yards out into the woods. I look down and see Sprite standing on her hind legs, front paws on her platform, with Paul's duck in her mouth. I help her aboard the platform and take the duck from her, and again she is zeroed in without want or need for direction from me. I watch her body language and where she is looking, and I can see that she is locked in on the first bird, floating dead in the decoys. The crippled bird is a hundred yards beyond.

"*No bird*," I tell her softly. "*Heel.*" She whines softly, prancing on the dog platform. I step over to the left of the dog platform and raise my hand near her head. I lean into her until she pivots away, and I give her a line with my hand until I'm sure she's locked on the cast I'm about to give. "Back!" I bark sharply, and she launches herself from the platform again, this time on a line about thirty degrees left of the bird in the decoys. She whines sharply, as if to say, "I *know* where the bird is, so why are you sending me *this* way?"

She passes twenty feet to the left of the dead widgeon, turning her head to look at it longingly as she swims by. I let her continue a bit further and blow a short blast on the whistle. Immediately, she turns to face me, treading water and watching me expectantly.

"*Back!*" I cast again, extending my right arm over my head, angled slightly to the right. Obediently, she turns again, swimming in the direction I pointed. Thirty yards further, and she veers off the line slightly and seems to hit another gear. She's seen the duck.

"God, I love watching that dog work," comes Paul's voice from behind me, his voice almost reverent. "She's...*perfect.*"

"Yeah," I reply softly without turning, trying not to lose sight of her through the trees, "that she is."

"Remember when we were kids, when your dad would take us hunting? Or all those times we hunted the potholes without a dog?" he continues. "Or hunting with that chocolate lunkhead Jason used to own? All those times, I thought that was duck hunting. It wasn't. That was just...shooting ducks. *This* is duck hunting."

He gets it. Maybe he isn't just a shooter, after all. Now he just needs to learn how to call.

Sprite eventually finds the duck and turns back. I can't see her, but she's making that peculiar snorting sound that comes from breathing around a mouthful of duck feathers. Presently, I can see her wake spreading behind her through the water, and her head appears as she clambers over a log.

"Not even seven o'clock, and four birds in the bag," Paul observes. "Not a bad start to the morning. So what's for breakfast?"

Rolling my eyes, I nod at my blind bag. "Hot chocolate in the Thermos, and goodies in the bag. Help yourself."

"Mucho grassy ass," he grins as he rummages greedily through my bag. He passes me a honey bun and a cup of hot chocolate, and we lean against my tree and silently watch the rising sun filter through the trees as we eat. Though the air is full of ducks, none of them are low enough to be of interest. Huge chevrons of migrating birds, pushed south by the approaching cold front. They're so high, they oughta be wearing oxygen masks.

"So when do the rest of the ducks show up?" Paul wants to know.

"Give it time," I advise. "Mallards are late risers. Kinda like you."

"So give those ducks a holler," he suggests, pointing straight up.

"*Those* ducks?" I snort derisively. "Paul, those ducks are so damned high, they're not even worth paying attention."

"Give 'em a holler anyway," he urges. "Let's hear the old Stuttgart highball."

"Dude, that's *contest* calling, and it sounds like a duck about like Sir Mixalot sounds like Bocephus."

"Do it anyway," he challenges, "That is, unless you're chicken."

Shaking my head resignedly, I take a deep breath, and cut loose with a long, eleven-note hail call, a series of notes that sounds like a duck to the uninitiated, but one that no duck makes in the wild. The effort leaves me breathless, and I take the call from my lips and take a sip of hot chocolate. "There," I start to say, "are you satis-"

"Mother of God," Paul breathes, staring at the sky. *"Look at that."*

I look up, and several chevrons of flight ducks have broken up, swarming chaotically in the sky like a cloud of gnats. As I stare in wonder, they wheel about, circling and losing altitude.

Jesus. Don't tell me I had something to do with that.

"Hit 'em again," Paul says, still staring awestruck at the sky. I consider telling him to put his head down, but I'm not sure ducks that high can even *see* a white face, much less be frightened by one.

I raise the call to my lips and call again, a six-note hail call this time, trying to make the notes raspy and insistent, like a bossy old hen *demanding* that they drop lower. Amazingly, the entire flock cups its wings and sails, rocking from side to side as they sideslip to lose altitude. More are above and behind them, doing the same thing.

"I ain't believing this," Paul exults as he wades quickly back to his tree. He pulls his cap low over his eyes and lowers his head, watching the wheeling flocks of birds without moving his head, looking for all the world like a demented Jack Nicholson as he rolls his eyes this way and that.

For the next twenty minutes, ducks rain from the sky. Flocks of twenty to thirty filter through the trees, sometimes alighting in the decoys for minutes at a time. Thousands more are stacked up at different altitudes, like airliners in a holding pattern at a busy airport. I've never seen anything like it. I only call sporadically, but when I do, the ducks wheel about as if I had them all on a string. By unspoken accord, neither Paul nor I shoot, and instead watch the show.

And a show is exactly what it is. God's pageantry on display.

Several large groups of mallards have settled in the woods nearby, and the hens have added their voices to the mix. I'm competing with real ducks now. After watching perhaps a thousand ducks pass within shooting range, I look over at Paul, and he just shakes his head in silent wonder. I make a crooking motion with my trigger finger, and he nods in agreement. We'll take the next couple of groups that we can decoy into range.

We'll have to. My dog is about to have a stroke watching all this.

I scan the wheeling flocks and focus on a group of twenty or so a couple hundred yards downwind of us. I raise the call and blow a staccato, insistent series of notes – a comeback call. As if I had commanded them telepathically, they wheel in unison and lock their wings, gliding into the wind as they approach our decoys.

I turn my head and hiss to Paul, "Big bunch on the left, cupped and sailin'. Get ready." I wait until the stragglers have their feet out, committed to landing, before I push away from the tree. I can hear Paul's sweet sixteen already barking as I shoulder my 870.

There, a drake just getting out of the decoys.

I watch him rise, my barrel almost languidly tracking him. Water droplets cascade off his feathers as he claws for altitude, and my 870 bucks. I watch barely long enough to see him tumbling over backward, as I shift to another target.

Drake, right over the edge of the spread, going away and rising. Take him now.

My 870 bucks again, and the drake folds, splashing into the decoys a second after the first. I lift my head from the stock slightly, looking for targets, and spot yet another drake rising above the treetops. A glint of silver flashes around his left leg. By the time I get on him, he's tall, but still reachable. I shoot my last round, and see him stagger.

Damn. I shouldn't have lifted my head.

"That one's wearing a Rolex!" Paul hoots, and I watch helplessly as he climbs out of range, wounded but still healthy enough to escape. A full second later, Paul's sixteen barks again, and the drake folds.

Damn, that was a nice shot. That duck had to be sixty yards.

I say as much to Paul, and he grins proudly. "Did you see the band?" he asks, excited.

"Yep. That's why I was shooting at him."

"You hit him. He was wounded when I shot," Paul offers. "I'll flip you for the band."

"Nah," I shake my head, "your shot put him on the water. The band belongs to you. That's the tradition." Actually, there's no such tradition, so far as I know. But I have duck bands, and Paul doesn't.

He does a quick count. "Five ducks out of that volley. Not bad shootin'!"

"Not bad at all," I agree, and send Sprite for the first bird. She picks up all five birds in short order, pausing only long enough to deliver the bird and lock onto the next duck. All I do is take the birds, give her the release command, and hang the ducks on the strap.

"She's like a machine," Paul chuckles, then does into a credible Michael Biehn impression. "The Duck Terminator, a cyborg. Cybernetic organism. She doesn't feel pity, or remorse, or the pain of having icicles hanging from her nipples...*and she will not stop – EVER! – until all the ducks are retrieved.*"

I laugh aloud at the thought, inadvertently blowing my whistle a bit, causing Sprite to turn around in mid-swim. "Good girl," I call to her. "Back!" She yips in frustration and resumes her retrieve.

When she comes back, she's carrying a hayseed brown duck from Paul's side of the decoy spread. I take the bird from Sprite and toss it to Paul. "Here you go, hen shooter," I call sarcastically. "I believe that one belongs to you."

Paul gives me the finger as he reloads his gun, and I chuckle as I watch the ducks mill about in the sky. Our volley rousted those who had lit in the woods, and now they were wheeling around, looking for a place to rest and feed. I watch them over the steam rising from my cup, and whisper quietly to my dog.

"Perfect, indeed."

THE REST OF THE MORNING WAS ANTICLIMACTIC, IF THE BEST DAY I'VE ever had duck hunting can be described as such. We killed our limit on the very next volley. Twelve birds killed with only fifteen rounds expended, and we were loading the boat by eight o'clock. There have been days before and since when I've killed many more ducks, but never a day so perfect as that one. Both of us hated for it to end, and so we drug our feet, taking the time to pick up our empty hulls floating in the water, lingering over the last of the hot chocolate and snacks before we finally clambered back into the boat.

All the while, birds were wheeling overhead, cupped and sailing until they were right on top of us. Some of them would land and swim around in the decoys. Others swam off through the trees. To this day, I can still picture it; shafts of sunlight filtering through the pin oaks, and swarms of mallards weaving through the branches, iridescent green heads shining in the sun as if the paint God had decorated them with was still wet. Their wings roared like a distant roll of thunder.

On the trip back to the landing, everywhere we looked, we could see ducks working. The crowd on Frank LaPierre Creek and the bean field was still hammering away. I wouldn't be surprised if every hunter on the river had shot their limit that day, but I doubt that any of them had been privileged enough to see what Paul and I had seen. At least, I hoped they hadn't.

Later, back at my kennels, Sprite and I dozed on the couch after a lunch of duck fajitas. The phone rang, and I answered on the third ring, "Chauvin Kennels."

"Where have you been?" my girlfriend demanded. "I've been calling you all morning! You didn't even answer your truck phone!"

"Paul and I went duck hunting," I explained.

"God, I don't know what you get out of standing around in freezing water before the crack of dawn, just for the chance to shoot a few stupid birds! It was twenty degrees at ten o'clock this morning, did you know that?"

"Honey," I smile patiently, "you just wouldn't understand."

"Whatever," she snorts dismissively. "Are you coming over tonight?"

"Yeah," I answer, "but I can't stay too late. It's supposed to be even colder tomorrow."

❦ 3 ❦

The Wolf Pack

By William Lehman

Hey, come on in to the camp, pull up a stump, and let me tell you the tale of "*the wolfpack*." All of it's true, only the names have been changed to protect the guilty (me) from the wrath of my hunting buddies.

Now, I guess it was about twenty years ago or so, because my daughter wasn't along on this trip, and Rob was still hunting with us, that we brought along Starbuck for his first hunt.

The leader of our little expedition was Buzz because he had been the most successful of any of us in actually dropping meat. It's worth noting that hunting Elk in Washington was a Low Probability of Success venture. Deer? Not so tough. Turkey? Again, not too tough. Grouse and upland game birds? Not a problem. Bear, if you know where to go, is very do-able... But ELK? Yeah, that's a tough one, especially if you're hunting state lands, (we were) and even more especially if you work for a living doing something that keeps you out of the woods, so scouting is hit and miss. That described all of us to a tee.

Washington's hunting regulations are designed, so they say, to maximize the hunter's ability to actually see an animal. Note that they didn't say anything about harvesting an animal. Most places were limited to either "Fork Horn" "Spike" or "True Spike" meaning no branching to the antler at all. The theory is that by keeping the older, big bulls safe, the herds will grow. They've been running on this theory for forty years, and the herds are still the same size... But hey, they're the professionals, we should just shut up and do what we're told. You get to see Royals, (7 point or better, western count) but you can't shoot them. It's sort of like looking into the restaurant, and watching the people eat.

Now the reason I called this group "the Wolf Pack" is because Buzz had this little saying: "A hunting party should be like a wolf pack. Fearless, relentless, and at the slightest showing of weakness by a pack member should turn and rend them limb from limb." (Figuratively speaking, of course.) It helps that three of the five of us knew each other through a Medieval Recreation Organization, and were all members of the same fighting group, so we "got" each other's humor. If you don't have a sense of humor, the first time your buddy puts you in the hospital with a broken bone from a hit at just the wrong angle, well, let's just say you don't stay in armor, and you probably don't stay in the organization. Anyway, I digress. (Pass the bottle this way, talking is dry work.)

So, since Starbuck had never been hunting before, and Buzz wanted to maximize his chance to actually bag something, we timed it to get the last weekend of Deer, and the first week of Elk. Bear is in season from before the start of Deer, until after Elk is over. As a result, we had a shot at three different species.

We all met up at the agreed-on camp site, and set up camp, then got the evening hunt in, before dinner. Camp consisted of a Travel trailer (mine) next to a fire ring, then a big wall tent, (Buzz's) a smaller wall tent, and a cooking fly, all across a small meadow "that was also the vehicle access/parking) from the trailer. This set up was driven by the layout of the site and finding enough level places to put everything up. Remember this layout, it will become important later.

Valder, the Norse God of the Hunt, has a checklist of the possible ways that a newbie hunter can screw up. Starbuck, being the over achiever that he is, was determined to get every box checked off on this hunt.

When we went out on that first afternoon, we spotted a beautiful 6-point whitetail crossing the road in front of us. So, we bombed down a side road to get ahead of him, pulled the rig over, parked ever so quietly, and with great care got out of the vehicle, eased the doors shut, checked our gear, and moved out in line abreast, hoping to spot that deer.

It wasn't more than 50 yards through the brush that Buzz held up a fist put his fingers to his eyes and pointed. Sure enough, through the edge of the brush, I could see the buck. Now this guy was no threat to the Boone and Crocket boys, he wasn't going to set records, but he was a respectable animal. 6X6 good strong main beams, and probably weighing in at about 210. Certainly, bigger than MY first deer, and honestly as big as the biggest one I have ever dropped. We held back to give Starbuck the first shot at him.

If I haven't mentioned it, Starbuck is a BIG guy, by which I mean both tall and wide. Yet, he managed to get through the brush with a fairly low level of noise. He got to within about 35 yards of the buck before the buck brought his head up and started twitching an ear... Took his rifle to his shoulder and we heard "CLICK."

Yeah, that's right, no round in the chamber. Guess which is faster, a newbie hunter cycling the bolt on a Model 70, or a buck who just realized he has an appointment on the other side of the state?

We spent about an hour beating up the area hoping to find him again, got one look as he bombed off the side of a coolie (that's PNW for canyon) almost strait down a good 400 feet. Even if I could have gotten a shot, there was NO way to get him back up the cliff. So, Critters 1, Starbuck 0.

There was some good-natured ribbing around the campfire that night of course... But, hey, newbie mistakes are called that for a reason, right? The next morning it was up way before dawn. I was making breakfast when a camp robber Jay jumped down on to my hot grill and took a big chunk of bacon off the grill flew up into the pine at the edge of the camp, and ate it. Well, I chucked a rock at him, and he flew down and took ANOTHER piece. That was enough of that, I unholstered my 45 and shot the little so and so, leaving him in the tree, "*Pour encouragement les autres.*" I take my bacon seriously! We spent the rest of the week unharried by Jays, so I'm guessing it worked.

After breakfast we headed out for the last day of deer season. We set up overlooking the edge of a clearcut, hoping to catch the bucks heading up into the high country after grazing all night on the verge. Just after first light, I saw some movement, it was too occluded to tell what it was, but it was headed for Starbuck. Soon we heard that distinctive sound that carries so well through the morning mountain air. "Ka-snick!" That was Starbuck taking off the safety. He didn't even try to gentle it. Needless to say, the buck, for buck it was, suddenly remembered an appointment over in Spokane. Score now, Critters 2, Starbuck 0, and Valder laughs and puts another check mark down.

We spent the rest of the day beating up the mountain, putting a lot of footprints down, and seeing nothing. Well, not nothing, we saw some beautiful countryside, and we kept seeing the prints of this one coyote. Same guy all over the 15 miles or so that we ranged. This guy was a freaking track star. By evening, we were all tired and frustrated. But tomorrow was a new day.

Next morning, Starbuck was too sore to go out, he volunteered to stay behind and be the camp B!&@h, said he would have food ready when we got in a little after sundown. Now I should mention that there was an ongoing competition in the WP for best meal made using all camp goods and equipment. This was SERIOUS business. We made mincemeat pies, lasagna, chicken enchiladas from scratch (and I use fresh scratch), all sorts of things... and Starbuck was known to be a great cook. So, everyone was absolutely all right with this deal.

Off we went. The day was semi unproductive, Buzz saw a royal, but he was alone, and the area was Fork horn or less. I got a look at the Coyote we had been seeing tracks of, came around a bend in the logging trail I was walking up, and there he was, standing right in the middle of it, 30 feet away. This guy was the biggest damn coyote I have EVER seen. Had to be 30 inches at the shoulder. I would have thought WOLF, but he had that long leggy big eared, bottle brush tail look that was distinctively coyote. I had heard the state biologists suggesting that they were breeding cross breeds up here in the cascades, and I believe it. I looked at him, he looked at me, and I thought about dropping him. But you can't eat Coyote, and he wasn't destroying my stuff (like that never to be sufficiently damned Jay!) plus if I shot him, any elk in the area would be headed for the Canadian border. After about three minutes of staring at each other, the Coyote flipped his tail, as if to say "well, if you ain't gonna fill your hand, I have better things to do!" and trotted off into the bush.

By 1330 or so, we were seriously up for some lunch. We headed back to camp, and grabbed some sandwiches, and some fruit then headed back out. The afternoon hunt was a complete bust. We headed back to camp and found Starbuck just coming back in himself, winded as hell, toting his rifle, and saying unkind things under his breath.

Well, of course, that required some explanations. It seems that He had left his rifle in his tent, and had gone over by my camper to lay a fire, when Mr. Bear wandered right through the middle of camp! Now I had two loaded rifles inside my camper, but Starbuck didn't know that, because he hadn't asked, and I hadn't told him. I always bring a couple spares if I'm going hunting for more than a day trip, this is the mountains, people fall, weather socks in to the point where scopes are useless, all sorts of shit happens. So, I had a second scoped rifle, and a 47/70 with iron sights within reach of the door. Little help that did Starbuck, because he didn't know it. What he DID know was that there was about 300 lbs. of bruin in between him and his rifle. So, he waited quietly, for Mr. Bear to waddle on out of camp, then ran over, grabbed his rifle and gave chase, fruitlessly for about three hours, before giving up and heading back to camp. Critters 3, Starbucks 0.

The rest of the week was like this. We all went out the next day, no one saw anything. Day four, Starbucks stayed in again, and drove down off the mountain to fetch some stuff from town, and make a phone call... Yeah, we were far enough out, there was nothing like cell service. He came back to find four sets of fresh elk tracks through camp. They might as well have left a note, "Hi, swung by, you weren't home, we'll try again later..." And Valder gets another check mark.

On the last day of the hunt, we had found an Elk superhighway. Starbuck wasn't up to walking much, the snow was knee deep on a tall elk, trudging through it was a bear even for someone in good shape, and he wasn't. It was about 15 degrees out, and you had to balance enough layers to keep from getting too cold, with not so many layers that you sweat. Sweating in this cold is a BAD THING ™. That way lies hypothermia. So, we put Starbuck on that superhighway, where he could see from where it broke over a ridge, to down through the valley and up the other side. This was the best spot we had seen. If he was going to see an elk on this mountain it was going to be here. Then we went out and beat the bushes, trying to see if we could get something up and moving. Maybe we get a shot at it, maybe we move it over to where Starbuck gets a shot...

About sixteen hundred, the sound of a single 30-06 split the quiet. Then a minute later a second shot. Well, that was about the right spacing for "down, followed by an insurance shot." We didn't go running though, we might still get a shot at something, there's another half hour of shooting light.

When nautical twilight hit, we came in. There was Starbuck, right where we left him, with a severely disgruntled look on his face, and no blood on his hands.

"Well?" We asked in full quadrophonic sound, "Was that you?"

"YES."

"So, where's the game?"

"See that Tree over there, about 40 yards away, across the logging path?"

"You mean the one that's broken off about four foot up?"

"Yeah."

"You didn't."

"I did. I saw him coming down the draw, and he was closing on me, so I waited to get a better shot. At about 45 yards, he was behind that tree, and stopped, with his neck and head sticking out from behind it, along with most of the front shoulder. It wasn't perfect, but it was the best shot I was going to get. He knew something was up, and was getting suspicious. So, I took the shot. AND HIT THE DAMNED TREE! He took off, and I tried a snap shot, but no luck."

The ride back to the camp was quiet. We had broken camp at lunch, so the only thing left was to load up the last of the stuff, check the lights on the trailer, and head for home. I was grateful that I wasn't sharing a rig with Starbuck and Buzz on the way home... I understand it was really quiet for the whole six-hour drive. Final score, Critters 5, Starbuck 0, but all his "newbie" screwups were covered. In his usual over achieving way, he had managed to make every single "newbie" mistake possible, in one hunting trip.

That Christmas Starbuck got four boxes of ammo, and 40 targets for Christmas... It seemed all of us thought the same thing... Although Buzz also got him a membership in the Rocky Mountain Elk Foundation, so that he would know what one looked like, "For next time."

Still, we were all back at it, next year, but that's a tale for another time.

❀ 4 ❀

Take the Shot

By Rick Cartwright

The fall that year had been unusually warm, so November still had a lot of fall foliage. Dad had gotten in from a trip late the night before, and so it was a little unusual seeing him at the breakfast table before I left for school that Friday morning. Putting down the phone, he took a sip of coffee and said in his best retired chief petty officer voice.

"We're going hunting tomorrow morning. Your great Uncle Bruce wants to thin out some deer on his pastures."

That explained the phone call at o'dark thirty. Great uncle Bruce had probably just finished milking the cows. So much for sleeping in tomorrow. I enjoy hunting and I loved the times I could spend with my dad. But tomorrow was the first Saturday after the end of football season and I had been looking forward to a lazy Saturday reading.

"Yes, sir."

The next day, it dawned bright and crisp. I got to drive. Crossing

Signal Mountain into the valley, I was looking forward to putting some meat into the freezer.

"Bruce was telling me last night that we should each be able to bag a buck today. He hasn't let anyone on his land since those idiots broke down his east fence two years back, so they're congregating in his fields and woodlots."

This was great news because we were stalk hunters. My dad's attitude was, " You'll get more meat going to the deer rather than sitting in a tree waiting for the deer to come to you. "

For me, stalk hunting demanded using all your senses. You have to be sensitive to wind direction, sound, and moving quietly through the woods. The biggest thing is to be quiet. If the deer hear you coming, they will be going. We didn't talk, communicating through hand motions.

By midday my dad had taken an eight-point buck which was field dressed and hanging from a branch of the ancient oak in my great uncle's yard.

"John, you and Ricky come in, warm up, and have some lunch. You might want to try up near the pastures along the old coal railway."

After lunch, we headed out. We followed some tracks along a game trail. There seemed to be a group moving together. One looked like a buck from the size and depth of the tracks.

That herd was like Jeffy in the Family Circus comic, wandering every which way. Then we lost them on some hard ground. I resigned myself to not getting a deer today. We came out into a clearing that I recalled overlooked the pasture nearest to Bruce's house.

"Well, that's something you don't see every day."

I looked where Dad pointed. In the middle of ten cows was the biggest deer I had ever seen. The buck had a huge rack. The amazing thing was that the deer was there at all. Deer and cows generally don't mix. No matter. That buck was mine. I raised my rifle to take the shot.

"I'm going to get that head mounted."

"Son. I wouldn't try that. Too much chance of hitting one of Bruce's cows."

"Dad, it's not going to be a problem using the scope. I know I can do it."

It was about a three-hundred-yard shot. Tough with iron sights, but definitely doable with my new telescopic sight. It was brand new, and I was so proud of it. I sighted the buck, putting the chest right in the crosshairs. It looked like a Field and Stream cover. I considered going prone, but didn't want to lose the moment. I sighted. Inhaled. Exhaled about half my breath instead of the full exhale people tell you. Dad taught me that to give you more time to line up your shot. It works. Not much wobble. I squeezed the trigger.

The buck jumped out of the crosshairs. The head of a Holstein took his place. My brain screamed at my finger to let go of the trigger. The next thing I saw was the cow tumbling out of the scope field. I lowered my rifle and hung my head.

"I am sure she didn't feel a thing, son. Looks like you need to talk to your Great Uncle Bruce."

My dad was never one for saying "I told you so." We walked back to the house in silence after getting the identification from the dead cow's plastic ear tag. I wasn't concerned about paying for the cow. I had the money. One nice thing about growing up in the trucking business was I made a lot more than most teenagers during the summers. It was still going to hurt. Milk cows weren't cheap. I steeled myself for a tough conversation and a depleted savings account.

A conversation I never had. Stepping up ahead of me on the porch, dad said 'Wait here."

About ten minutes later, dad and Bruce emerged.

"Ricky, hook up the drop gate trailer with the winch to the John Deere and pull it out. " My great uncle directed.

Shortly thereafter, I chauffeured my kin to the pasture, glad the wind had shifted so their cigarette smoke was blowing away from me. We passed the herd as they placidly made their way to the barn, unconcerned about their missing fellow.

I got the carcass on the trailer as my father and Bruce supervised. Ten minutes after we pulled in front of the house as dusk was falling, a refrigerated truck that had started life as a milk truck judging from the lettering and the image of a regionally well-known bovine that white paint hadn't completely obscured pulled up. The bold red print of "Jack's Meat Shop" identified its current owner. Jack Travis ran a small packing house locally supplying his butcher shop across the mountain in Chattanooga along with processing game. He was also a part time game warden. He checked Dad's deer in and took it as well.

"Won't need a tag for the Holstein," Travis quipped.

My father blandly asked, " Jack, you know a good taxidermist? Ricky mentioned he wanted to mount the head."

"I changed my mind, " I said through gritted teeth.

Everybody's a comedian, I thought as my elders chuckled.

I turned to my great uncle after the refrigerated truck's tail lights disappeared in the growing gloom.

"How much do I owe you, sir? I can go to the bank after school Monday and drive the cash to you. "

"The cows are past time for milking. You remember how to milk a cow, boy?"

"I think so, sir."

Surprisingly, my dad joined us as well. With the three of us, it went quickly. I felt like I was being sent out to cut a switch, as I was wondering just how much my bad shot was going to cost me. Bruce only talked to the cows while he was milking and the suspense was killing me.

We put the last of the raw milk in the cooler.

"Thank you both. Let's go inside and talk things over."

As soon as the door closed behind me, my great Aunt Mary piped up,

"John, you and Ricky sit down to dinner with us. I made plenty and there's a cherry cobbler in the oven. Ricky, I know that's your favorite."

"Mary, don't mind if we do. Let me call Frances"

"Dad, I bet momma already started dinner. Let me settle up with Great uncle Bruce and we can be on the road," trying to hide the desperation in my voice. My great aunt was nearly as good a cook as mom and I knew we weren't going to have cobbler at the house. Plus, I know she was trying to cheer me up. But I was desperate to know how much that cow was going to cost me. If we sat down to dinner, then business was going to have to wait till we were done.

I turned to ask Great Uncle Bruce for a dollar figure. He held up his hand.

"Ok honey. We can have it tomorrow. Enjoy your salad."

"Tell Fanny that I will send her a plate. She doesn't need to lose weight!" Great Aunt Mary called out from the kitchen.

Dad hung up the phone after passing the message. "Your mother got in from the store late and was going to pressure cook some pintos. This will let her soak them overnight and simmer all day tomorrow. See if Mary needs any help to set the table."

Another hour rolled by. Finally, Bruce tossed his napkin on his plate, took a sip of coffee, grimaced and turned toward his wife, who was topping off dad's cup.

"Mary, is this decaf? "

Really? God, what did I do to deserve this? Come to the point, I silently begged.

"Bruce. You know what the doctor said. You need to watch your blood pressure."

Harrumphing, he turned to me and said. "I know you want to know what you owe me. I also know that you are saving for college. So I will not take your money."

Relief coursed through me.

"But," he continued, " I do expect you to come here all day Saturdays and Sunday afternoons to work off the value of the cow. Ten or twelve weekends ought to do it. Your daddy tells me you get up at five thirty to get to school. So let's say six thirty to evening milking Saturday and one in the afternoon to milking time on Sundays."

"Bruce, that's the Sabbath." Mary interjected.

"Dear, the cows have to be fed and milked every day. Not to mention mucking the stalls. If God intended farmers to have all of Sunday off, cows wouldn't shi..."

"Bruce!"

So that was my weekends till the first week in February when I became the proud holder of a bill of sale for one Holstein cow. I looked at that bill of sale for years thereafter at the start of every deer season as a reminder to be very careful about my shots.

And as the late, great Paul Harvey said, "Now for the rest of the story."

Five years later, my dad's cigarette smoking caught up to him as lung cancer. At the wake, Great Uncle Bruce pulled me aside.

"Ricky, remember that cow of mine you shot a while back?"

I looked at him, puzzled. "Yes, sir. I think I still have calluses from shoveling... " I caught myself," muck."

"I told John that I had already called to send that cow to Jack. She had dried up about a week before. Your daddy talked me out of telling you and came up with the idea of helping out on the farm. You were a big help." He saw the question in my eyes.

"Why did he do that?" Bruce continued. "He wanted to make sure that you had a reminder to be more careful hunting in the future. But he also wanted you to know that you can't always buy your way out of trouble. That's a big lesson son and I hope you will remember it."

Bruce walked away.

I looked up at the heavens and smiled.

❈   5   ❈

Snake Stomp

By Regan Smith

By Regan Smith

A**uthor's Note:** *This story came from my grandfather, who often talked to me about his cowboying days. He was particularly fond of his horse, Dexter, when he worked for the TO Ranch near Raton, NM. He was also fond of telling stories that may or may not be completely true. I wrote this one as best I can remember the way he told it.*

I SUPPOSE NOBODY LIKES RIDIN' DRAG, 'SPECIALLY IN JULY. BUT AT least I was ridin' drag on some horses that day, 'n the dust weren't near as bad. It had rained a coupla days back, a fair lot, so the dust was tolerable. Dexter was kinda skippy that day, so I sung to him a bit before the dust got on my tongue, 'n' he settled down.

We wuz fixin' to start the TO Ranch roundup, 'n' bringing in all the horses first. I wuz about six months shy of bein' the foreman, but that's another story. Fer now, I wuz just another hand – well, not really, 'cause I knew how to repair all the tack, so I wasn't out on the range near as much as the other hands. I kinda liked bein' out, but when yer the best at repairin' tack, guess where yer gonna be?

Anyway, Dexter 'n' me wuz bringin' up the rear, when alla sudden the lead horse, Whitey, screamed bloody murder and went nuts. He wuz a-stompin' and rearin' like a rodeo bronc, and the other horses spooked and run off to the west. The other hands rode after them, but Dexter 'n' me stayed with Whitey to see what he'd do next.

Well, we finally got a good look see, and Whitey was busy killing the biggest rattler I'd ever seen on the TO. Whitey never did like any snake, but when he saw a rattler, he just went to war. Now Dexter wasn't real fond of snakes, neither, but that day he stood still and watched Whitey, 'stead of joinin' the stomp. If he had, my job woulda been ta hang on and not git in the way.

WHEN WHITEY FINALLY CALMED DOWN, THERE WUZ JUST A GREASE spot in the grass.

Best snake stomp I ever did see.

Biggest Catch of the Day

WHEN I WAS ABOUT TEN, OUR FAMILY, MOM'S TWIN'S FAMILY, AND Mom's brother's family all went to Monument Lake near Trinidad, Colorado for a vacation. Two things were particularly special about that: first, we were going on a vacation without visiting family and staying with them for free, and second, we'd never done a multiple family vacation. So that's why I remember this one so well.

At the time, the big rock formation from whence the name came was still out in the middle of the lake, and there was a big mostly rock beach from which we did all our fishing for the rainbow trout stocked there.

We stayed in log cabins that probably dated from the 1930s, nestled underneath so many trees that it was semi-dark all day long. Each cabin had a woodburning stove and screens nailed to the inside walls to keep bugs from coming through the holes between the logs – a good part of the chinking was missing. I don't remember much about the cabins except the woodburning stove and all the screens, and the fact that we had to carry water from a central pump and use outhouses. That, and the best tasting biscuits I ever ate came out of that woodburning stove. Mom wasn't the best cook in the world, but she knew her biscuits and how to do it in a woodburning stove.

Anyway, a few days into the trip, I'd stopped fishing the day before, mainly because I don't like to eat freshwater fish and the rule was "You catch it, you clean it, you eat it." So I was wandering around the beach edge far from the water, looking for pretty rocks to take home. I'd just bent over to pick up a little rock when my shirt tried to strangle me.

Uncle T.J. was doing a lot of casting into the lake, aiming at the rock formation out in the middle. I think he was practicing his fly-fishing technique. Well, his line flew way back behind him and he caught a big one. Me. The hook was firmly embedded into my shirt, which got dragged up around my neck.

Took my dad and Uncle Pete a bit to untangle me from my shirt and the hook. I wasn't even scratched, but my shirt was holed up pretty good.

Uncle T.J. got ragged about his big catch the rest of the trip.

The Huntingest Cat Ever Known

HIS NAME WAS ALEXANDER THE GRRREAT, AND HE WAS THE GREATEST hunter in the world.

In late October 1996, a friend and former co-worker called me at work. One of her co-workers had found a kitten hiding under a bush, yowling loudly. As a dog family, they had no idea how to handle a boisterous ball of energy that climbed draperies, thought their dachshund was a pony to be ridden, and insisted on copious amounts of affection and head bumps.

Rather than just dump him by the side of the road, as the father was planning, my friend said she knew of a safe place for the little guy. She called me and asked if we could take a third cat. I discussed it with myself for about five seconds, told my friend we'd take him, then called Spousal Unit to advise we'd be adding another cat.

Her co-worker's entire family brought this tiny tuxedo cat to his new home. As they opened the carrier, I asked their young son what the kitten's name was. "Gidget," he replied. Oookay, that's probably not what the cat thinks his name is. About ten minutes after he arrived, it was apparent that Tuxedo Kitten's name was Alexander the Grrreat, for he conquered house, cats, and humans with dispatch and affection.

The little guy strolled right up to our oldest cat, Klaus mit der Krallen, who hissed without any real venom, then sat down and watched Alex explore the den. Heidi HiDee Ho, our long-haired tabby, decided on the spot that Alex presented a threat to her relationship with Klaus, whom she loved dearly. Klaus was oblivious to her affection, but Heidi maintained a frosty relationship with Alex the rest of her life, not that he noticed much.

The previous family had been feeding him dog food, so when we put him on kitten chow, it took about six weeks for his little body to make the proper adjustments. To say he was gaseous is a serious understatement. He could melt eyelashes and clear blocked sinuses with that stuff. His nickname, "Fart," stuck for life, even though he was far less likely to grace us with more of the same after the initial break-in period.

Alex never met a human he did not love. When I was sick or down, he stayed by my side. He even insisted on inspecting my abdominal staples after a surgery, by walking on them before curling up in his favorite spot – on my chest.

Getting to the hunting part of this story, in the short time he was with his mother, Alex learned how to hunt and how to manage humans. He was the most efficient killing machine we ever knew. He was prepared to show his humans he could take care of himself and bring them food, too.

Alex' hunting technique was somewhat unusual for a cat. Instead of stalking his prey, he burrowed under leaves and waited for it to come to him. When it got close enough, Alex exploded out of the leaves and landed on it. We saw him in "action" more than once – it was amazing to see, if occasionally kinda slow.

The first few times he proudly brought home his catch (baby rabbits) and presented it to his people, we took it away and let it go. After that, he made sure whatever he brought home had its neck broken before presentation.

He was so prolific that our neighborhood often asked to borrow him. This is an important point, so pay attention here.

A new family moved into the court, in the middle house down at the circle (we lived on the corner). Mom came storming to us one day, loudly declaring that our cat had "murdered" the baby rabbits in her yard, and her children had "SEEN IT!!" (cue heart palpitations, pearl clutching, and general apoplexy.)

"Were these your pets?" I asked gently.

"No, they were wild."

"Then I don't see the problem. This is normal here in the suburbs."

Well, she sure didn't like to hear that. As she started a rant I happily do not remember, Alex strolled around the side of the house with a baby rabbit in his mouth. He dropped it at my feet and started to bathe.

"Aren't you going to save it?" she ranted.

"Nope. It's gonna die in about...it's dead."

She declared us monsters and stormed away. Alex ate his rabbit tartar in peace.

A few weeks later, the court had one of its periodic potlucks down in the circle, right in front of her house. She spent a good bit of time glaring at us and whispering to her non-court-resident friend. Her immediate next-door neighbor strolled up to us, and in a loud voice said, "Hey, we have a chipmunk problem. Can we borrow Alex?"

"Sure. We'll stroll down with him later."

"Great. He's the best rodent control I've ever seen."

I don't think Ms Non-Congeniality ever talked to her neighbor again, either.

We never mentioned that we thought Alex might actually have been highly active in the Federal Chipmunk Relocation Program, as we'd seen him play catch and release with various critters before finally dispatching it. Spousal Unit actually saw a chipmunk get away from Alex and scamper up a tree. We're sure one or two others likely got away.

Talk about a cat on a schedule – Alex definitely had one. Spousal Unit came home one day, let Alex out the front door, then went upstairs to change clothes. When he got back downstairs, Alex was on the front porch with a squirrel. He ate the entire thing, except the tail and guts, then immediately demanded his dinner be put down. He didn't necessarily want to eat it right then, but it was dinnertime and dinner bloody well better be there.

Alex' last kill took place only two weeks before he died. We were at Mom's, caring for her after she t-boned her car into a pickup, broke her knee, ankle and two ribs, and totaling her car. Alex was just sitting on her deck, enjoying the warm for January day, when a bird landed on the deck railing right in front of him. The bird was there, then it was on the deck beneath his paws, and he'd already broken its neck. Someone opened the deck door and he brought it inside before we could block him. He argued with us but finally consented to eating it outside.

We almost lost him due to eating the string off a roast and years later catching pneumonia, but our savings account, veterinarians' determination, and Alex' own fierce survival skills brought him through each time. Finally, at the human equivalent age of 98, Alexander the Grrreat was called to the Rainbow Bridge, Hunter Division, where, on 20 Jan 2017, he met up with his best friend, Klaus, and all the lovely lady kitties who shared his home over his life.

RIP, Alexander the Grrreat, my heart kitty. I love you.

⚜ *6* ⚜

"A-Moose-Ing" Alaska Stories

By La Vaughn Vanderburg Kemnow
(First published in Alaska Bush Mother)

Charged by a Bull Moose...One fine autumn day on the Alaskan homestead I went out to my garden to pull turnips to add to the moose stew I was planning for supper. When I stepped outside the cabin, I saw two bull moose facing me a short distance away, at the edge of the yard. This didn't startle me as they were frequently around the cabin. I had enjoyed watching them from time to time throughout the summer whenever they came to visit. They had never been aggressive in any way, and I considered them to be my friends.

As I walked toward the garden, the moose (two-year-old twins) slowly turned and started walking away, down the hard-packed dirt driveway. Then one turned right, the other turned left, and they disappeared among the trees.

The turnip tops were long, thick, and crisp, and I decided to remove them before taking the turnips inside. I would pull a turnip, grasp it with my left hand, twist off the top with my right, and drop the turnip into a brown paper bag.

As I was engrossed in the task at hand, I was startled by a sudden, loud, and menacing snort. I quickly looked up to stare into the eyes, less than six feet away and at about the center of the berm, of one of my moose friends. He had been attracted by the juicy sounding "snap" of turnip tops being twisted off.

After looking me over for what seemed an eternity, but was probably only a few seconds, the young bull moved rapidly to the end of the berm and around it into the garden, facing me with no barrier between us. He snorted loudly several more times, then advanced toward me a few feet at a time—not running but prancing, snorting, and shaking his head.

My first tendency was to run. However, I didn't think I could outrun a moose. I briefly considered grabbing the tines of his antlers to keep from being speared by them, if he got that close. I had a fleeting unwelcome fantasy of being thrown onto his back and trying to stay on as he galloped through the woods. I also considered climbing onto the berm. He could reach me in the center from either side, but if he went to one side I could move to the other. Since the berm consisted mostly of loose brush, rather than soil, the moose would probably not be able to climb up onto it.

A more important consideration, however, was that my three small children were also in the garden. I couldn't just run off and leave them at the mercy of a wild animal bent on destruction, to possibly get trampled by those big hooves. I called to the children, who were near the row of peas on the other side of the garden, to run to the cabin. Once they were safely inside, I could decide on a course of action (or non-action) for myself.

They looked, saw danger, and ran as fast as their chubby little legs could carry them—toward me, not to the cabin. Mother represented safety to them. They hung tightly to my legs. As the moose advanced, prancing a few feet at a time and shaking his antlers at me, I stood my ground. This was a young moose, but the points on those huge palmate weapons he carried on his head looked ominous to me.

I yelled at the moose at the top of my lungs, and shook my bag of turnips in his face. The children joined in the yelling.

He came closer, in spurts of frenzy, dancing a jig as I continued yelling and threatening him with my bag of turnips—the three little children, Kathleen, four years old; Douglas, three; and Mark, two—pressing against my legs.

Then the moose stopped a short distance away, still shaking his head and snorting.

Finally, apparently deciding we weren't worth the trouble, he turned and jogged away a few feet at a time, still prancing and turning his head to look back every two yards or so, sometimes turning a complete circle to look at us. When he got to the far edge of the garden, I slowly herded the barefoot children toward the cabin. I was anxiously looking back over my shoulder every few seconds to see whether that young curious moose would charge again

But was it just curiosity—or was he becoming aggressive because it was the beginning of rutting season? Or perhaps he didn't like the idea of my making moose stew, with or without turnips!

The next day, I worked up enough courage to go back out to the garden, warily trying to look all directions at once—armed with a tape measure. Just twenty feet from my footprints in the soft brown garden soil were those of the moose; and that massive hardware he carried on his head would have been several feet closer.

Moose Canning Camp...Moose was our main source of protein. We had fresh moose, frozen moose, and canned moose; fried moose, moose roast, moose tongue, moose stew, moose heart and liver, moose gravy, moose dressing, moose made into patties, ground moose loaf, Swedish moose-meat balls, more moose—and I never got tired of moose.

One Fall my parents came to visit, and wanted us to go on a hunting trip up the Denali Highway, toward Mt. McKinley.

I rarely had a chance to go on outings, and was glad of the chance to go. So we loaded up our camping gear, went up the highway—a rough gravel road—hoping to get in a year's supply of moose meat.

The men made a successful hunt and brought the moose—two big bulls—back to camp. And then the work began!

As it was during the early moose season, in August, and too warm for meat to keep for very long, we had come prepared to can the meat. My parents had purchased cans and lids from one of the seafood canneries on the Kenai Peninsula, and had a hand-operated device to fasten the lids tightly to the cans.

We started early on moose canning day. It is generally recommended that meat be processed in a pressure cooker. That was not possible in our situation; we had to use the water-bath method, which takes a lot longer.

Our canning kettle consisted of a fifty-five-gallon oil drum with the top removed. Very early in the morning my father dug a deep, narrow trench for a fire pit, and settled the oil drum securely over the pit, leveling it at the bottom with flat rocks where necessary.

He then filled it about one-third full of water from a nearby creek, and built a fire in the trench underneath. The next step was to put up a long trestle table, with boards set on makeshift supports—old oil drums that had been left behind by construction crews. We then placed sections of moose on the table to be cut up.

As my father cut meat off the bones and kept the fire going to bring the water to the boiling point, my mother and I cut the meat into small pieces, discarding scraps of fat and membrane, and packed the meat into the cans. We set the filled cans in pans of boiling water on a camp stove before sealing the lids, in order to make sure they were hot all the way through before going into the drum of boiling water.

Because of our makeshift method, we boiled the sealed cans longer than the specified time, to be sure they got hot enough. This was an all-day process, and not to be recommended, but it worked for us—we ended up with several hundred cans of moose meat, all properly sealed, and never lost a can to spoilage. Primitive but effective.

While busy with the moose canning operation I had to keep an eye on Kathleen, and frequently dashed off to bring her back when her unbounded curiosity took her too far afield. There was a small creek nearby, and that was a magnetic attraction for her. And at that age (sixteen months) she never walked—she ran!

Several times during the day I lifted her up onto our meat table so she could watch us work—until she got squirmy and needed to be put down to run some more. Baby Douglas, two months old, slept most of the time in our tiny travel trailer.

Late in the evening, with the cans all filled, sealed and in the processing bath over the fire, we were tired, hungry and ready to sit down and relax

Dad had started a small campfire earlier which had produced a good bed of hot coals, He had sliced, salted and peppered some tender moose backstrap, and cut forked green willow sticks.

We threaded our steaks onto the willow forks and slowly roasted them over the hot, glowing coals, enjoying the aroma almost as much as we enjoyed eating the steaks—a perfect ending to a busy, productive day.

HUNTING MOOSE IN MY FLANNEL GRANNY NIGHTGOWN...ON August 20th one year, the first day of the first moose season, I got up at first light—3:30—shook myself awake, and staggered to the door in my long flannel patchwork print granny gown.

There was a young bull moose in the yard, feeding at the haystack we had for the cow. He just stood there staring at me, no doubt wondering what kind of creature I was. The .270 was by the door, so I used it. It was too heavy for me, and I was so sleepy the sights looked fuzzy. I shot him three times before he went down.

I'm sure it was the same moose I saw the day before in the edge of the lake, by the garden. When three-year-old Douglas saw it, he yelled, "Hey, moose! We're going to shoot you tomorrow! 'Cause the season opens tomorrow." And he told me the moose said it was all right.

Four-year-old Kathy got up and dressed herself—except for shoes— and came out to "help," but she wouldn't touch the moose. She was very interested in the blood veins, heart, liver, and intestines. What's this? What's that?"

About 4:30 Doug poked his head out and said, "There's a moose in our garden!" We thought he was talking about the one we were dressing out, but he wasn't; there was another bull in the garden. That moose went into the woods.

The children's father left to help a neighbor with some mechanic work while I cut my moose in seven pieces and managed, with much grunting and groaning, to manhandle them one at a time into Doug's little red wagon; then hauled them over the rough ground to the other side of the cabin and hung them in a tree. Good strength training!

Camp robbers—Canada jays, or grey jays—can be pesky critters. One persistent jay started stealing big chunks of my moose! After numerous failed attempts to chase it away, I shot it. It was unlawful to shoot camp robbers.

The Game Warden had his boat moored on our property, at the edge of Clearwater Lake. The day after I shot the moose, he came out to patrol the local waters. While I was talking with him, Kathy came skipping up to him and said, "Mama shot a robin." Then Doug ran around the corner of the house with the camp robber and said, "Mama shot it! Mama shot it out of a tree yesterday!"

The Game Warden didn't say anything, just smiled, and I asked him if we weren't supposed to shoot them. He said they are a nuisance, but they didn't encourage it; and something about "as long as you have a license."

TO SKIN A MOOSE...ANOTHER YEAR, MOOSE SEASON HAD ARRIVED, and it was time to restock the larder. The men, of course, had done their share of providing meat for the table. They had killed a big bull moose.

Instead of hanging it under the trees to cool, they hung it on a tripod where there was no shade, in front of my in-laws' house. It was late September and we were experiencing an exceptionally warm and sunny autumn. On my way to the store for groceries, stopping to see if my in-laws needed anything, I found my mother-in-law pacing around, worrying herself sick about the possibility of the meat spoiling. It was not covered, the hide had been left on, and flies were buzzing around it.

She couldn't handle heights, and would experience dizziness if she climbed a ladder to skin the moose.

I had no trouble with heights, and had quite a bit of experience with a skinning knife, so I dragged the heavy, homemade ten-foot-high A-frame ladder over, set it up, climbed to the top, and went to work.

It took about an hour for me to remove the hide from the animal, most of the time on the ladder with my right leg wrapped around the ladder frame so I could safely lean far out to the left to do my skinning. It was awkward and slow work.

My mother-in-law paced below me, making worried comments and wringing her hands. Before I descended the ladder to do the lower part of the skinning, she brought me a box of pepper to sprinkle on the upper part of the moose, to discourage flies.

She then went back into the house and found an old thin bed sheet. After finishing the lower part of the skinning, I went back up the ladder and fastened the sheet around the moose carcass, to keep flies off and to keep the sun from shining directly onto the meat.

A job well done. We could now cut off pieces of meat to take into the house to cook or to cut and wrap for the freezer.

One reason my mother-in-law had been so worried, while I was up on the ladder, was that I was more than eight months pregnant (with twins, as I found out the next day when I went to a doctor).

$\maltese$ 7 $\maltese$

There Might Be Such a Thing as Too Much Gun...

By Kat Stevens

I t's a bit of a cliché in the gun world to say a particular weapon is "too much gun." Some people say it when referring to their belief a gun is simply too big while others use it to reference the fact that there's really no such thing as too much gun. As a general rule, I fall in the category of a shooter who believes there's not a single firearm on the entire planet I'd consider to be excessive. That goes for caliber and overall size. Bigger is better, right?

At this point in my hunting career I've fired a ridiculously wide range of guns at a crazy number of game animals, predators, and varmints. There was that time I took a Desert Eagle chambered in 429 DE on a turkey hunt—hey, it's legal in the great state of Texas—and that other time I used a Barrett Model 82A1 out calling coyotes. Full disclosure: There were other times and other guns. I tend to lean toward large calibers.

There was one time my gun was quite possibly a wee bit much, though. Well, twice.

The more memorable event took place during a turkey hunt in North Texas. It was a work hunt, meaning I was using an array of new or newish firearms for the purpose of writing about the hunt and how the guns worked. Among what I fondly remember as a beautiful array of firepower from Magnum Research, there was a BFR—that's Big Frame Revolver, get your mind out of the cussing gutter—chambered in 50 Linebaugh. This particular revolver was one I'd had my eye on since my friend and fellow gun writer Jeff Quinn first started talking about it (sadly, Jeff has since passed, leaving a massive hole in the heart of the gun industry). I decided hunting Texas during turkey season with it was a fabulous plan.

On the day in question, I was sitting in a pop-up blind with the Magnum Research BFR in 50 Linebaugh in my lap and a rifle in the corner—this was Texas, after all—and a box call in my hand. I was pretty thrilled with that box call, because I'd just had an amazingly cool double on turkeys in South Dakota using it. For the turkey and gear-obsessed, the call in question was a Rocky Mountain Turkey Strutter I'd gone ahead and used black chalk paint on to fine-tune the sound. It was awesome.

Back to the blind. There I sat in the admittedly toasty April weather, listening to turkeys sound off all around me. I knew they were there; I'd already shot birds with another gun (the rifle) on another day. One specific Tom had captured the majority of my attention. He was hung up somewhere in the mesquite behind my pop-up blind. Ever so often he'd gobble and there would be snaps and clicks as he either strutted or tripped his way through the dry brush. That meant that ever so often I'd perk up, believing his stubborn tail was getting closer.

This went on for some time. The back-and-forth was killing me, and my frustration was growing. Dusk and dinnertime were also approaching, and my guide for the hunt—who would eventually become my husband, but that's a whole other story, and at that point I was too dense to notice—was texting me that he was on his way to pick me up.

Our texts went something like this:

Me: "No! Don't come! He's getting closer and you'll scare him off."

Him: "Okay..."

<Five minutes pass with total silence.>

Me: "Might as well come, he's gone."

Also me, ten seconds later: "No, wait! There he is! Don't scare him!"

Him: "Okay I'll wait."

<Five more minutes pass. Silence.>

Me: "I give up, just come get me."

Him: "On my way."

Me, two seconds later: "NO NO NO! He's coming!"

This went on for some time and I'm probably lucky my guide didn't tell me exactly where to stick my frantic texts. Meanwhile, the turkey in question wasn't actually getting closer. He was just messing with me, because turkeys are evil. They have tiny, beady little eyes, smooshy faces, and crabby personalities.

Finally, I gave in and sent the text okaying a noisy diesel truck to come rolling into my setup. That's when the raccoon wobbled into view.

Now, you have to understand that raccoons are a serious menace on farms and ranches. They destroy farm equipment, dismantle feeders, and eat turkey eggs, among other things. The property I was hunting was massive and free range, so really, that bug-infested masked bandit could have gone elsewhere. He had tens of thousands of acres at his disposal, all of which he could've used to leave me and my turkey-free setup alone.

He was waddling out in front of me. I knew he was a pest, one most places want disposed of. My trusty 500 Linebaugh was in my lap.

50 yards. 25 yards. 15 yards.

Possibly, it would have been wiser to shoot him while he was further away. After all, a 50-caliber bullet meeting a raccoon is bound to be a colorful experience.

I was frustrated. That turkey had hung up on me for quite some time. It was hot, I was tired, and there was an equipment destroyer in front of me. One that ate turkey eggs.

Without hesitating, I brought the 500 Linebaugh upon target and pulled the trigger.

Two things about the BFR 500 Linebaugh: It fires bullets that are .510 inches in diameter and it's beautifully precise. Sure, the recoil is on the punishing, but it's worth it. Right?

One moment the raccoon's furry butt was there. The next it was gone.

Had I seriously missed a raccoon at 15 yards? This, I thought, would be a horrifyingly embarrassing story to tell. Then I heard a tell-tale crash —which was a little odd, because it was a rather large clearing—so I got up to look.

There was an extremely large, bold, bright blood trail on the ground. I paused a moment to text my guide, but instead of "got a raccoon" what came out was "so. Much. Blood."

Yes, he made it there quickly.

I was already across the clearing, having followed the blood trail— which was more of a blood road—to the source of the crash. The 500 Linebaugh had impacted the raccoon hard and hot enough to field dress it and fling it across the clearing into a mesquite tree. It was, of course, gone to meet its forefathers in the great corn bin in the sky.

It's worth hitting the pause button to mention that one reason I like big bore guns is because there's no doubt they'll get the job done. None of this undersized bullet garbage; you just know a magnum or otherwise huge bullet is going to drop your target on the spot. The 500 Linebaugh definitely fell into the category of "effective."

However, the raccoon was basically vaporized.

There is a possibility using a 500 Linebaugh against a trash panda is… excessive. Maybe it's even too much gun.

Today, his skull is resting on my dresser. As a reminder of what was a stellar hunt, but also as a visual check on my gun choices. Ask yourself this: Sure, I like big guns and I cannot lie, but is this one maybe…too much?

Be honest. It just might be.

Facials Mean No Euros

It was the scene of my daughter's first hog hunt. We were in Mississippi sitting in an elevated stand, her waiting with breathless anticipation, me waiting and praying a willing tribute appeared before darkness fell. My daughter Grace was only 12 years old, but it wasn't her first hunt, simply her first time going after feral hogs. She'd enjoyed the meat-based fruits of my labor from my own hog hunts, so it seemed like a good plan to get her on one of her own.

Grace was armed with a gun that remains a favorite of mine to this day, a Remington R25 GII in 308 Winchester. The rifle has a nice camo pattern but it's downfall is the short Picatinny rail, which doesn't really allow for much in the way of accessories. It did manage to fit a Bushnell Legend Ultra HD 1.75-5X 32mm optic I had sitting around, so I'd mounted the scope to the rifle before we hit the road for our hunting spot.

I'm definitely one of those hunting parents that doesn't just mention safety in passing, I drill it in until my kids are beyond sick of hearing about it. That means Grace had heard the usual questions, repeated the typical recitation of safety rules, and spent time practicing with that specific rifle. She'd zeroed the optic herself, nodded and sighed when I got repetitive with my instructions, and made the necessary snack selection when we hit a local grocery store.

Coca-Cola? Check. Nutty Buddy? Check. Sour slime and other assorted squishy sweet things? Double check. All we needed was a hog. Just one hog.

I no longer remember how long it took for one to appear. The Johnson grass around the blind was extremely tall which made it difficult to see anything, especially with the wind moving the blades in a teasing manner that made you think something was there when it was not.

It's strange hunting with your kids when you yourself aren't in the hot seat. On one hand, you desperately want your child to be successful. The last thing you want is for them to be skunked. On the other hand, you'd rather be doing the shooting yourself, and omigod what if the most epic 500 pound albino Hogzilla ever strolls out in front of her and I have to let her shoot it?

Grace, of course, had prepared herself for whatever might happen. She'd watched a ton of YouTube videos, which lead to the unfortunate belief that any hog that we came across would charge us, maim us irreparably, and leave us for dead, and she'd stared at shot placement charts. Did she want the hog? Yes. Was she convinced it was some sort of vampiric porcine demon out to get us, no matter what I said to the contrary? Also yes.

Dusk was falling when a cloven-hoofed tribute finally appeared on the scene. I know this because photographs of Grace with her first hog back up the time of day. In all likelihood, she was more chill than I was;

Grace had the rifle resting on the open window sill of the blind, shouldered snugly, eye on the target.

I, on the other hand, was absolutely panicked she'd miss and get nothing.

He wasn't a big boar, maybe 120 pounds at the most. His hair was bristly and brown, so nothing stunning or cool to look at, either. What he was, was her first chance at shooting her very own hog which she would then get to eat.

There was a narrow window of time when the boar crossed a tiny open spot in the grass. Compared to the vastness of the acreage around us, it was miniscule at less than ten feet wide. He wasn't alone; there were three pigs—cue Three Little Pigs jokes—trotting across the path.

She took the shoot.

The Remington Hog Hammer ammo did its part of the job, and the hog went down.

According to my handy rangefinder, the deceased member of the Three Little Pigs had been 125 yards away when she shot it. It looked like an ideal shot, and when we processed him, we discovered she had, indeed, made a perfect shot through his heart. He was gone before he hit the silty dirt.

As I mentioned before, this was not her first hunt. She knew what to expect, knew there was movement after death. Even so, she panicked.

What if he wasn't really dead? What if he was suffering? What if she only wounded him, and he was twitching in agony?

By that point we were on the ground standing over him. He had assumed room temperature—figuratively, of course, since his body had yet to cool—but Grace was worried. To soothe her worries, she asked me to shoot him myself to make sure.

This is where I tell you what gun I had on me.

Because I was not the one hunting and wasn't concerned with much, I'd resurrected an old favorite. It had been my very first carry gun years before, and every once in awhile I liked to bring it out. The gun? Well, it was a Glock 27, meaning it was chambered in 40 Smith & Wesson. Say what you will, the 40 Smith & Wesson is a great little cartridge. It's understandably fallen out of favor at this point, but there was a time when it was The Cartridge to Have. Because I'm nostalgic—and because this particular Glock 27 once saved my life—I kept it.

Thinking only of ending Grace's worries over the (dead) hog's potential (death tremors) suffering, I drew my Glock. Several rounds of 40 Smith & Wesson met feral hog skull.

"There," I told her. "He's definitely dead."

Now, hours before, Grace had informed me she had no desire to get any sort of mount done of her first hog. She didn't want a shoulder mount, which was unsurprising, but she also did not want a Euro. That was fine. It was her choice.

Her first hog was field dressed, dragged to my truck, and taken back to the little cabin we were staying in. In no time at all it was processed and divided into freezer bags, all the better for me to take home and process for real.

It was as the boar's carcass was about to be delivered to the bone pile that Grace spoke up. She'd changed her mind, and she wanted a Euro of her first pig so much!

This was not good news. You see, a handful of bullets from a 40 Smith & Wesson all but guaranteed there was nothing left. Oh, he had a skull, but fitting it back together wouldn't even be puzzle-like, it would require great imagination. Was it a hog? Was it a zombie alligator? The taxidermist never would have known.

And so, I had to explain that when mommy had mag-dumped into her hog because Grace herself wanted to be positive it was dead, all hope of a Euro had been lost.

Have you ever watched your child's face fall in disappointment over a lost dream, all while knowing it was technically your fault? I have. Mommy and her Glock 27 destroyed that boar's skull quite effectively.

Since that day, Grace has shot other hogs (and deer, etc). She still has no hog skull Euros although she does occasionally pick up a sun-bleached remnant of some long-forgotten pig that died from old age or a mafia hit. I still feel bad about that one. Semi-auto facials mean no Euros.

8

Los Lobos

By Carolyn Taylor

I heard barking and went to the windows which were across the back of the living area and gave a view of Tom Cove which lay past the lawn and beyond the line of cedars. There, standing with a paw on the trunk of a cedar tree was Mick, head stretched toward something in the branches. I smiled at the young Irish setter's exuberance. I sensed a movement to the left, and changed my view, almost simultaneously whispering 'Oh my god.' No more than twenty feet away a magnificent coyote was looking back at Mick, and as I gazed, turned and took a few steps back toward him, mildly curious. He was so – what? sophisticated, I imagined he might have thought to himself, 'Silly young whippersnapper.' He turned back and strolled away. I remembered to breath.

That afternoon I thought of an adventure taken years ago.

My husband and I were perhaps ten miles or so from the town
of Durango, Mexico, in an Olds 88 driving on an almost non-existent
road through barren land. With us was a man, an American who had
lived in Mexico for many years, roaming around doing whatever he did.
As we bumped and surged over small ditches, cactus, rises, and rocks we
made slow progress. A sinister noise caused us to stop the car to see what
had happened. The car had pulled up a weathered stump by its undercar-
riage. A worried view upside down showed no damage, and lurching and
bumping we drove on.

A large lake attracted our attention as thousands of Sand Hill Cranes
clouded from the skies onto the water as we were passing. A few hours
into the journey we approached a tiny village, no more than two or three
adobe huts. The men approached an old man sitting on his heels by his
open door and asked if there was any Tequila about. Nodding his head,
he rose and entered the tiny room and brought out a mason jar of what
he called tequila – it tasted like kerosene. It was added to the small box
holding a few onions, jalapenos, pinto beans, and coffee.

We pushed on, miles and hours. There was no one, no sign of life.
Our guide, McAnnaly, who'd roamed around Mexico for years had picked
up many dialects of Spanish. Somewhere in the vast countryside we saw a
man leading a burro. Stopping to ask directions, McAnnaly couldn't
understand the dialect and could not make out what he said in answer to
his questions.

There was nothing to do but push on. Though it seemed very
doubtful that we would ever find our way. I, at this point thought we
were completely lost. We did make our way to the camp in the 'boonies'
in the late afternoon.

A dip in the landscape, a few trees shading a small stream, which we
easily forded, and two or three adobe and weathered wood buildings and
we had found our destination. There were only a few women, a man or
two in view, steadily going about their daily chores. Our guide appeared,
greeting us, and escorted us to our accommodations.

Our wooden cabin had bunk beds and rudimentary cooking facilities.
A bathroom? – no. My husband was quite good with the language and he
and McAnally chatted mixing English and Spanish. The men had had a
difficult conversation, many hand gestures, with our guide, and we were

to saddle up and hunt the next day. I spread my bed roll on top of the wooden bed and slept fitfully. "*Si! Lobos – grande.*"

After a meager breakfast – was it only coffee and a morning wake-up of tequila? – we mounted horses and set out across a large plain towards the mountains. Drifting back to me the conversation between the three men was barely intelligible to me with my newness to the language. The few words I knew included two that were sinister. "*Lobos*" and "*Grande*" The men had rifles slung over their shoulders. I had no rifle.

Gaining the foothill, we followed a narrow trail with the right side beginning to fall off ever deeper. So much talk about Lobos and how Grande they were. The deer were sparse due to the Lobos.

Moving ever higher along the side of the mountain I began to be aware of each step my horse took. A quick look ahead as I heard the rattle of small stones disturbed, didn't make me happy. Rain had washed out the trail creating a bit of a jump for the horses. My mind fought against this maneuver, but my horse was in the momentum of his kind and with a short little jump we were quickly past the eroded area.

The trail wound around the mountain as we searched for any sign of life. As we rode, an image in my mind had grown so that I had expected at any turn to look up and see a monstrous wolf, with blood dripping from its jowls. There was no wild life, not a bird or rabbit. Nada. We gave up the search for deer when high, high up, and began to descend through the heart of the mountain.

I was riding a pony before I was able to walk well, advancing to ever larger animals. I was not shy of doing tricks on horseback, and letting one run full speed. I had not ridden for several years and never on a mountain trail. We came to a low stacked wall. I dismounted after noticing that the terrain became ever steeper on the other side. Mounting the horse on the other side of the wall, it took only a few yards to convince me that I would be sliding forward onto the horse's neck, or so it seemed. I dismounted again and was barely able to stand much less take steps without sliding on the fallen leaves. With great trepidation and difficulty, I mounted the sturdy horse, and again felt the disconcerting idea that saddle and all were going to slip forward. Knowing that my horsemanship reputation was in jeopardy, I tried my best to play it cool, and at last we were back on the level plain.

It was approaching noon, we were tired. I swung my leg over the saddle horn to rest. The words *"Lobos"* and *"Grande"* no longer resonated in my mind. The men were in front, single file, my husband in the middle. He looked back at me, several yards behind him, and proceeded to rest as I was, lifting his leg across the horn. I felt proud of my 'city' guy, who was not the rider I professed to be. He looked strong and like a cowboy with his Western hat and his rifle slung over his broad shoulder. Now that my fears were behind me, I was happy.

We were enjoying the ride, looking forward to getting back to camp. The unfenced land was nice and flat and here and there groups of trees broke the landscape. The first group of large trees was reached. The peace was broken suddenly by a muted sound of scuffling hooves. Horrified I saw my husband falling − still in a half yoga position jerked off the saddle as the horse tucked his withers in fright when the rifle caught on a low limb. His fall was so quick he landed as he had been sitting, on the horse, his leg arched over the saddle. He sat for a bit. I was thinking, "My God! We are hundreds of miles out in the boonies. What if something is broken?" Much relieved, I watched him rise, with nothing more than his pride damaged. Sorry, but I couldn't stop myself from giggling.

We thought about food. All the fresh air and exercise had made us ravenous. The few women in the tiny village were busy. The men went to talk to them and found they were cooking a turkey to make their Christmas tamales. They came back and asked me about buying some. Oh no, I said. That was the only thing they had to eat.

We cooked the beans. With the onions, jalapenos, and a shot of tequila they were pretty darn good. Not as good as they would have been if accompanied by venison liver and onions. The *lobos grande* had evidently already eaten Christmas dinner.

❧ *9* ❧

Head Shots

by D.L. Campanile

(Names and details have been redacted to obscure the guilty.)

A couple of brothers went deer hunting with their dad and their new brother-in-law. Nobody particularly liked the new guy, but hey, he was family now, might as well get to know each other.

They each had a 30.06 or a .308, scoped, very nice ones. He'd been lent a spare. They'd been telling him hunting stories since they'd met him, and this was his first hunting trip ever. After a long day of slogging through the brush, only to head back to camp empty-handed, they spotted a wild rooster up in a tree, next slope over. Not looking forward to the hotdogs in the ice chest, they decided a poultry dinner needed to be in the offing.

"Chicken stew for dinner, boys?" Dad asked, to a general nod of assent.

First brother shot, missed. Bird fluffed up its feathers a bit, but otherwise didn't seem particularly bothered. Next brother, same thing, then dad. They missed too.

Now, brother-in-law, who had been convinced that they were all either great shots, or lying through their teeth, was a bit confused by this outcome. After all, target practice generally went very well for all of them, and he struggled to compete. The idea that every single one just missed a stationary target did not make sense.

Nevertheless, he was the last one to try, so he stepped up, aimed carefully, and shot. The bird disappeared in a cloud of feathers.

"We were shooting for the HEAD, you jackass!"

The hotdog dinner was a rather silent affair after that.

❧ 10 ☙

Duck Hunting Along the Brazos

By L.A. Behm II

Growing up, we hunted duck. Dad and several of his friends would get a lease somewhere along the flyways in Central Texas, and we'd get up oh so freaking early and drive out to some spot in the middle of nowhere to haul a couple hundred pounds of gear – guns, snacks, decoys, something to sit on, and thermos loads of hot cocoa and or coffee – to a wet blind.

Because the blind was always wet. It might not have rained for weeks, and it might not rain in Waco, but the blind would draw water like a sponge. Every. Damn. Time.

We hunted two basic locations – stock tanks on local ranches, or a lease that fronted on the Brazos River. The process in both, unless we were jumping stock tanks, was the same – I and my brother, if he were along, would end up in the blind, setting things up, while Dad put on his hip waders and went to set the decoys.

This, of course, is when Dad would find the hole in his hip waders he'd sworn to fix at the end of the last hunting season. He'd swear to fix it when the season ended again. As far as I know, those hip waders ended their days with that same pin hole in them. There was always something that kept the old man from fixing them.

If we were hunting the Brazos, he'd hop in the boat and set the decoys while I ran the cows out of the blind. Seriously – there was supposedly no way for the cows to get in the blind – it was about six foot high and eight feet long, but most mornings I'd be chasing some semi-feral cow and her calf out of the blind through a hole that had been built specifically to keep cows out, according to one of Dad's hunting buddies.

Cows are, in my experience, evil beasts. There's nothing quite like finding a sixteen hundred pounds of pissed off Angus cow in a small space and having to gently chivy her out of a small space – firing a round was generally frowned upon, and killing the cow was out of the question – all in the dark.

Then, of course, part of setting up in the blind was looking for . . . fresh cow patties. Dad had a thing about stepping in cow patties, and removing them was a priority. Dad, however, didn't want to carry anything vaguely military while hunting – which meant no folding e-tools, canteens or any of that stuff. Have you ever tried to pick up wet cow shit with a stick? After I stood up to Dad – I've been told he and I were butting heads on a lot of things from an early age on my part – I started carrying part of my camping gear when we went hunting – which meant a pistol belt, suspenders, WWII aluminum canteens, a 1960's military butt pack, and a Belgian folding entrenching tool. Cow patty issues went away for the rest of the season.

Once everything was set up, it was time to wait for the sun to come up. Once the sun came up, the real fun began. I don't know if you've ever been duck hunting, but in some ways it's a lot like combat – long periods of boredom punctuated by moments of excitement. I've done both. Duck hunting is . . . healthier long term.

Dad started his days with a cup of coffee, and would have a second and third on the way to the lease. Once the decoys were set, he'd have another one, to warm up – either because his leg was wet, or because the wind was blowing down on the river.

Coffee leads to calls of nature, which is where this story is going, if you haven't figured it out.

The old man carried a Savage Model 28 twelve gauge to hunt. It was built before shotguns were restricted to three shots total for hunting water fowl. Dad solved this problem by taking the gun apart and cutting down a dowel until the gun would only hold two shells in the magazine. I was briefly upset by this – he got the dowel from my Houston Astro's pennant.

As an aside, that bit of dowel is still in that gun – and is the only physical reminder of that trip to Houston still in my possession.

Because I was young, my gun was a Brazilian made single shot twenty gauge that my mom's dad picked up for thirty bucks in a pawn shop in Copperas Cove.

I'm sitting in the blind, watching the sun come up. Shotgun is broken open with a round in the chamber. Dad leans his gun against the front of the blind and opens his combination seat, ammo can and supply box, pulling out the partial roll of very important paper, muttering something about needing to see a man about a dog. I waved a hand in acknowledgement, and went back to watching the sun come up over the river. Astronomical twilight gave way to nautical twilight, which finally gave way to civil twilight. Just as civil twilight became dawn, there was a whistle of wings and a loud, authoritative "Quack!" followed by splashes as a pair of ducks flared and landed on the edge of the decoys.

"Dad," I stage whispered. "Ducks."

Mumble, mumble was the response.

"Ducks," I whispered louder.

Mumble, mumble, mumble.

Fuck it, I thought, closing the action slowly. I'd give it one more try.

"Dad, Ducks!"

Mumble, mumble, mumble, MUMBLE.

I thumbed the hammer back and rose, just as the ducks figured out they had set in with some strange, plastic things – and decided they needed to continue their voyage.

You'll hear things like it's more sporting to shoot them on the wing. Yeah, that's sporting and all that, but it doesn't put meat on the table.

I caught the first duck as the wings came up.

"What the fuck is going on?" Dad shouted; "Did you drop your gun?"

I hit the release on the trigger, snapping my shotgun open. The ejector tossed the spent casing hard – it bounced off the roof of the blind, and hit dad in the face as he came through the door.

He'd pulled up his underwear, but he had one hand on his belt, holding up his pants.

I closed the action on my shotgun and pulled it back up to my shoulder, thumbing back the hammer and tracking the second bird, which had lit the afterburners at this point. Things went into that perfect picture, and I dropped the hammer the second time. The bird dropped like a rock.

I opened the action a second time, this time catching the spent casing as it popped out of the chamber.

"Ducks, Dad," I said, pointing at the river.

The second bird went floating past, headed for the Gulf of Mexico. Dad saw it go past, and went out the front of the blind, down the bank of the river and into the boat, pulling up his pants on the way.

"There's two," I shouted at his back as I closed my gun on an empty chamber.

One of the rules we operated under was no guns live when someone was on the water. We might miss birds, but no one was going to end up like that lawyer who went hunting with Dick Cheney in 2006.

Downstream was easy – scull a couple of times and snatch the duck out of the water. The second bird had hung up in some brush on the bank. But Dad was a good ways downstream by that time, and he had to row against the current to get back to the blind.

I got to hear about rowing against the current all the way home.

❧ I I ❧

Fish Story

By Clair Kiernan

I don't fish.

That's a strange way to start a fish story, but it's true.

I don't like to fish.

I like being on the water, watching the play of light and shadow, enjoying the fresh air and sunshine, all that communing with nature stuff —but I don't need to fish to do that.

In fact, handling smelly, slimy, squishy things and stabbing my thumb trying to impale a worm adds nothing to my day. Baiting hooks was always my job when I was a kid, and mom would drag me (my brother Gary went voluntarily; just another way we were nothing alike) to the nearest damp spot on the ground so she could sit and not move or speak for hours.

I found it incredibly boring because I was six years old and had to sit still and be quiet. If you talk or shout, you'll scare the fish. If you run around and play, you'll scare the fish. If you stand anywhere near the water, they'll see your shadow and it will scare the fish. If you skip rocks, not only will you scare the fish, they'll pack up and move to another pond somewhere else, apparently, judging by how mad Mom got.

Then when we got home, I had to help clean the fish. I can't imagine why my mother thought that would win me over.

But I'm the weirdo in my family—me and dad, that is. Mom, my brother, my grandparents, aunts, uncles and assorted cousins all love hauling poles and tackle and bait to the most inaccessible places on the water. (Not the spot most convenient to the cabin or road, mind you, or the most scenic, or the place in the shade where the breeze blows the skeeters away.) Fish seem to congregate along muddy banks too steep for a chair, where rocks and overhangs mean you're more likely to get a bite from a water moccasin than a bream. If you're in a boat, that giant fallen log where the King of the Largemouth Bass holds court will be smack in the middle of the lake, where a blistering sun beats down on glassy water innocent of the slightest breeze.

I may be the weirdo in my family, but I'm also the sane one.

A while back some years ago my brother-in-law Steven, who unlike my husband likes to fish, came down from New York for a visit. He and my brother and my mom all got together and decided that they wanted to go fishing out at my cousin Butch's place. Even if my husband didn't have to work that day I was going to be outvoted, so I tried to lose graciously.

Daniel smirked a little as he left for work.

I told my mom, "Fine. I'll drive us there. I'll carry your chair and fishing tackle and cooler and fetch you cold drinks. But I'm not going to fish. I'm not going to touch slimy things. I'm not going to clean fish. I don't fish."

I wasn't sure what I could do with myself all day sitting around while the others went fishing, but I really hoped it would involve air conditioning.

We went over to Butch's place. Back then he had a sod farm just east of Covington. He worked for the phone company and bought himself a sod farm that he and his kids worked on the weekends. They put a couple of ponds on it that he stocked with fish.

I kept my end of the bargain, although frankly I didn't see the point in trying to fish in the middle of the day in summer. Anyone could tell you the fish weren't going to be biting much in the heat of the day. I drove the car out to Covington and beyond to my cousin's farm. Presently my brother Gary and my brother-in-law Steven were launching a small aluminum boat out to the middle of one of the ponds and ready to catch fish. My mom set her chair up on the bank in a shady spot. The first thing she did was hand me the pole and say, "Here, put a worm on this hook for me."

I looked at the pole. "I don't touch squishy slimy things."

My mother didn't move; she just kept holding the pole out.

So, I put the dadgum worm on the dadgum hook and I handed her the pole and I went back up to the house to wash my hands and get some Bactine and a band aid. I figured I'd be better off staying in the house until lunchtime, so I talked with Butch and his wife Jane while she puttered in the kitchen.

After I ate lunch—a hot dog and Coca Cola, if you're curious—I began to wonder how the others were getting along. I went down the hill with a cold drink for Mom.

The path between the house and the pond was not part of the farm proper. Weeds and scrub trees and bushes grew tall and thick on either side, so I could hear voices before I could see anyone. My brother and my brother-in-law were not having a good day.

"Look," my brother Gary insisted, "we should be fishing right over there. Can't you see? That spot right there. That's where the fish are."

Steven sighed. "We just got to this spot. I don't want to move. We're not going to catch anything in this pond anyway. I just want to stay put and be quiet and enjoy myself."

"No, we need to go over there. There's a hole."

"Hey! Watch it!"

"See? Look where I'm pointing. That's where all the fish are."

"Will you just sit down—" Steven was interrupted by a splash.

I decided not to ask them how it was going.

Over on the bank my mom was contentedly leaning back with one leg hooked over the other, her foot swinging gently. She didn't care whether she caught anything or not. She had a couple of puny bream on a string. At this rate if we wanted fish for dinner tonight, we'd have to stop at Long John Silver's on the way home.

I saw my mom's line go taut so I dropped off the Coke and quickly left before she could foist more dirty work onto me. I consider needing more than one band aid per day to be a bad thing.

I went back up the hill and reported the lack of progress to Butch. He considered for a moment, and said, "They ought to try the other pond. You know, that one's got bass in it. Maybe they're biting today."

So, he grabbed up a large bag of something that looked like dog kibble although I didn't ask him what it was, and we went down to get the others.

I helped Mom carry her chair and stuff, and we all went over to pond number two, which was just a short walk away, but there was no boat in this one.

Gary, still dripping, gave up in disgust and went up to the house. Steven planted himself on the bank and baited his line with grim determination. Something in his expression said that being at work was looking better all the time.

My mom found a new shady spot for her chair, still happily not caring whether she caught a thing. For her, catching fish was not nearly as important as going fishing.

Steven pulled his line out of the water and examined a small fish. Too small to bother cleaning, it was about the right size for bait. He gave my cousin a skeptical look. "Are you sure there are fish in this pond?" He was trying not to say not only are there no fish in this pond, there are no fish in this state or south of the Mason Dixon Line. It is all a lie.

Butch took a scoop of kibble and spread it across the water like he was sowing seed, and about two seconds later a line of bubbles came boiling up from the bottom as big mouth bass snapped and snatched and attacked that kibble, and then sank back into the murky darkness. My brother-in-law stared, open-mouthed. "Should I be using that on my hook?"

"Nope," Butch replied. He picked up a rod and reel, baited a worm on the hook, and casually tossed the line into the water. In less than a minute he had a bite. Because he was a good host, he offered me the rod instead of reeling it in himself.

"Clair, you want to reel him in?"

"Okay, sure," I said, twirling the handle and pulling back on the rod.

It took a little more effort than I expected, because a largemouth bass weighs a pound or two. Butch deftly removed the fish and re-baited the hook, then handed the rod back to me and pointed.

"You see that shadow right over there? See if you can drop it right near that log."

I plopped the hook in pretty close to where Butch pointed, and in a minute or so my bobbin took off for the antipodes.

Steven gave me the sort of look that precedes the end of diplomatic relations, followed by a declaration of war. Or, in isolated rural areas, homicide with no trace of a body. Luckily, I had my big cousin standing right there for protection.

I reeled in another largemouth bass and Butch baited the hook again.

"Have at it," he said with a twinkling grin, handing back the rod and reel.

I swung the hook into the water again without really aiming for a particular spot. But I wasn't terribly surprised when in just a couple of minutes I got another bite.

I looked at Steven and felt terribly guilty. Grinding his teeth in that manner could only cause him pain and suffering in the future. And besides, although I was Butch's guest, he was my guest. I hope I know how to be hospitable.

I walked over to where he was sitting and pretending not to notice me.

"Steven?" I asked sweetly. "Would you like the lucky rod and reel?"

I can't remember his reply. That's my story, and I'm sticking to it.

I don't want to say any more about the rest of the day because it would sound like bragging, and since I don't fish does it really matter how many fish I caught?

We feasted on fish and Mom's hush puppies that night. Butch cleaned all the fish, and the ones we didn't eat he froze and sent home with us.

After a while Steven started speaking to me again, although sometimes he twitches a little when he looks at a fishing pole and sees me in the same line of sight.

So that's my fishing story and it is almost completely true. I don't fish because it wouldn't be fair.

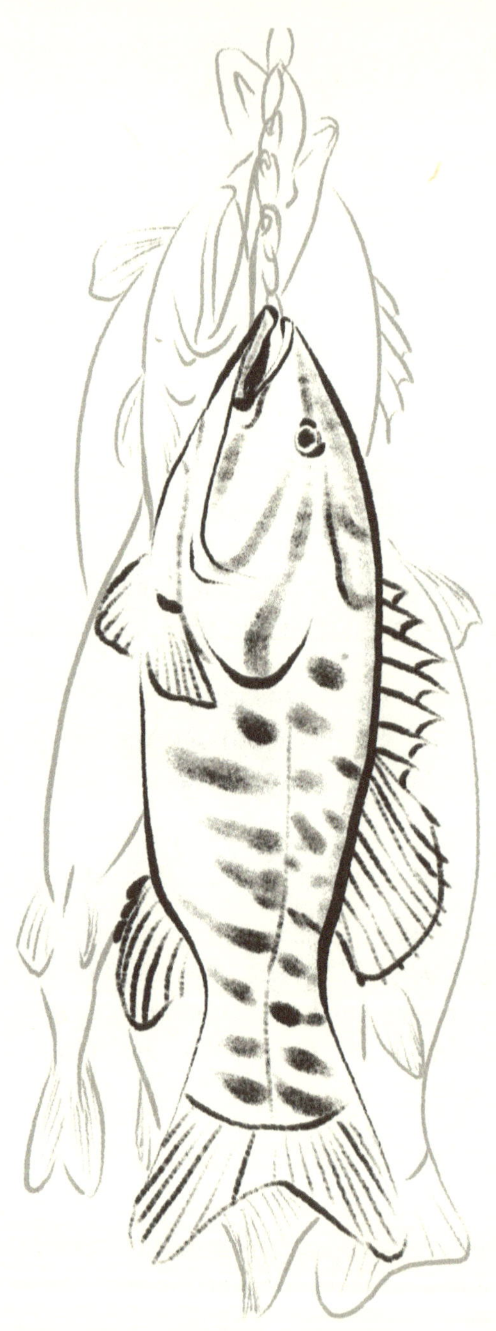
Cedar

❧ 12 ❧

The Great Goose Hunt

By Shauna Hicks

My family mostly hunted deer and elk. However, pheasant, quail, grouse, and waterfowl were welcome meals also. I grew up with three older brothers, a younger sister and we all hunted as did my mom and dad.

My middle brother Denny often ended up as the one stuck "watching" the girls. One day shortly after my oldest brother Mike had shipped out to Viet Nam my mom took my sister and next older brother shopping in Klamath Falls, an all-day affair. Denny is left in charge of me. Denny like honker hunting more than the rest of us and he decided a nice goose dinner would be just the thing to get mom's mind off Mike shipping out. Well, he can't leave me home alone although I WAS almost ten years old! I had passed my dad's requirements to pack a gun to hunt and had my first deer hunt that fall. So, Denny says we are going goose hunting. I adored my brother Denny...still do in fact...so I readily agreed.

It was COLD. Wet snow and sleety rain falling, light wind, muddy snow on the ground. Denny had spotted a big gaggle of geese down low on The Flat when he was doing chores. The Flat...a large low spot with heavy clay soil, salt grass, grease wood, wild rye, and some other types of bunch grasses about a mile from the house. Why the honkers seemed to love that flat is still a mystery to me.

We prepare for the hunt. Now Denny doesn't want me to get cold, so he gets me dressed up warm. Too bad we weren't going to Antarctica because I was dressed for it! Finally dressed, day packs with emergency stuff, guns ready, instructions given again and again... keep my muzzle up and watch I don't foul the barrel, be quiet, lead like I had been taught... and covered with socks to keep the barrels clean we start walking the mile to The Flat. After about 30 minutes of walking in the heavy clay soil I could barely pick up my feet. I am sweating inside my heavy clothes; I itch and have already drunk all my water; I think I am getting a blister. Denny was afraid I was making so much noise I would spook the geese, so he had us dropped into the drainage ditch that went the length of The Flat. Hunched over just like Denny although my head was at least 2 feet below the bank we made up time being hidden. There was enough water to wash some of the thick clay off my boots, but I am waning fast. I want to go home, but I can't show weakness to Denny, or he might not let me go next time.

Denny decides we are about even with the geese. After many whispered instructions, threats, tips and all those things big brothers tells you we are ready to hunt. He boosts me up on top of the bank. Hands me both shotguns and climbs up next to me and takes his gun back. We take the socks off the barrels, assume the army belly crawl position with guns cradled in our arms we start our sneak. My arms are on fire from the strain. Water is soaking into my pants and my boots feel like cold lead. Slowly we crawl and crawl and crawl. Denny whispering instruction and I don't know what else because I have long since frozen into a barely moving semi solid block of wet clay.

NOW!!! Shouts Denny! We raise up to our knees and...NOTHING happens. We had just put the biggest, coldest sneak on a gaggle of Deeks! Decoys! I wanted to shoot them just to make a point!

I don't think I ever went goose hunting with Denny ever again and seldom with anyone else. I'll just eat turkey...

Cedar

❧ 13 ❧

HOW (NOT) TO HUNT THE SKUNK

By Peter Grant

In 2003 I was living in North-Central Louisiana. It was interesting, because the local wildlife was convinced that they own the neighborhood. Humans were just intruders on their territory. I had an armadillo nest underneath my house at one time, and other wildlife tried to do the same thing at frequent intervals.

A family on my street had seen skunks wandering around and warned me to keep an eye out (my house, like theirs, had a crawl-space underneath, and we both used wire and other barriers to stop animals getting in). One Saturday morning they detected sounds of movement beneath the kitchen and an interesting smell was in the air. Dad checked underneath with a flashlight and found that two skunks had moved in.

He went out that afternoon to talk to a nearby zoo about removing them (they do a lot of that sort of thing). Unfortunately, (!) his teenage son decided he'd show Dad that he was able to handle the problem. He duly took Dad's .22 caliber rifle, lay down next to the house, inserted the rifle through the hole in the wire netting through which the skunks had entered, pushed his head and right arm and shoulder in through the hole, lined up the sights and let fly in the skunks' general direction.

Bad move. Bad, bad move.

Not only did he miss the skunks, he blew a hole in the water pipe leading to the hot-water supply. Water began to spray all over. To add insult to injury the skunks apparently didn't like the noise and sudden shower. Both of them let fly in the direction of the shooter, scoring simultaneous direct hits. The boy was, of course, unable to back out of the way in a hurry, having got hung up on the wire around the crawl-space.

Dad came home to find his son sitting on the front porch with the door and all windows firmly locked; his wife and a plumber trying to sort out the water leak; and half the neighborhood (including yours truly) gathered round making helpful suggestions about how to wash skunk smell out of the boy's hair (to say nothing of his clothes and the rest of his body). The son's girlfriend, with whom he had a "hot date" scheduled for that night, arrived soon afterwards. She took one whiff of his *'eau de col-ugh!-ne'* and informed him that she'd changed her mind!

When I went out for supper that night Dad was planning on buying several catering-size tins of tomato paste and forcibly bathing his son in a tin tub in the back yard. This was a good idea in theory, but was shot down by the fact that the water supply was still switched off until the plumber could repair the pipe! His wife informed him that it would be a divorce matter if 'his' son came back in the house smelling like that.

I came back that evening to find the family gone. The plumber had refused point-blank to get under the house to repair the pipe until the ghastly smell had been removed. Since no-one could figure out how to get rid of it without running water, the family spent the night in a motel - all except their teenage son, who was banished to the back of their pickup truck (which had a camper shell), with a sleeping-bag. He was eventually able to scrub down with tomato paste under a tap at the rear of the motel, but judging by my nose was still in need of treatment the following morning.

The family spent the next day trying to remove skunk odor from under the house with the aid of hoses from their neighbors. They went through eleven large spray bottles of Febreze: one on their son, seven under the house (interspersed with copious amounts of hose water) and three indoors on their floors and furniture, which had become permeated with *Eau de Skunk*. The under-house treatment allowed the plumber to get under the floor later that afternoon and replace the shot pipe.

Their son was at last allowed back in the house, but he lost his shooting privileges, allowance and a few other things for the next year (and boy, did he feel sorry for himself! - but he had the grace to admit that he deserved it). His girlfriend allowed him to take her out the following weekend, but she warned him in advance that he'd better be smelling like a rose!

And the skunks? They disappeared during all the fuss and weren't seen again. They were probably rather miffed at having their cozy romantic nest disturbed like that. Who invited these noisy people into their neighborhood, anyway?

⚜ I4 ⚜

A Snow Lake Skunking

By Kermit Grenoille

If you look at a map – or GPS, let's face it, this is the modern age - of the state of New Mexico (yes, we ARE a state, thank you very much, and no, I do NOT need a passport to go to Oklahoma or Massachusetts – although sometimes I do wonder about the latter), and pan around the southwestern corner of the state, from the Rio Grande west and south of Albuquerque, you should look for a label saying "Gila National Forest." Yes, it's a weird word; it's pronounced "heel-ah" and is Spanish or something. Call it "gill-la" or "jill-la" and we'll know you're not from around here. Anyway, start looking through the national forest for a small, high reservoir named "Snow Lake." That is where we shall be going for this trip. No, there's no paved road. It's all dirt forest roads. I hope you have four-wheel drive. And maybe a tow rope. And a chainsaw, in case there's a blowdown of beetle kill across the road. The Forest Service tries to keep the road clear, but they don't always get to a deadfall in time. Now...

My first fishing trip took place when I was six years old. If you know how old I am, then I don't need to say the year this happened. If you can't figure out the year, I won't tell you, because then you'll know how old I am. Ahem.

My grandfather, or "Pap," as we grandkids all called him, grew up in the backwoods of rural and dirt-poor Appalachia, and he needed to hunt and fish to survive, often without the blessing of the game warden. Once he grew up, he made good and could afford to pay for licenses and fees and tags and such, but he still enjoyed listening to the robins singing the news, or fetching some venison for the table, or sitting on the banks of a lake or stream and napping under the pretense of catching some trout for the table. His son, my father, was rather less "woodsy," but had grown up going with Pap on his hunting and fishing trips, and was very much in favor of my being exposed to the same, and deciding if I liked it for myself or not. So, while I grew up in Big City, smelling exhaust and hearing oompah music and rap blaring from open windows along with cigarette smoke, my vacations from the age of six onward were more often than not spent with Pap and Grandma, going off and doing Outdoor Stuff. The trip to Snow Lake was only the first of many. But this story isn't about all those other times. It's about Snow Lake.

Pap had planned a big family get together of a bunch of men in the family (and their wives, those who would tag along at least), and I was invited and included. Dad, for reasons I don't remember if I ever knew, stayed behind, but I carried my parents' blessings, a brand-new Walmart fishing rod I had no clue what to do with, and a tiny tackle box with three bobbers, a little plastic baggie of lead sinkers, and two packages of hooks. In contrast, Pap had at least two giant tackle boxes. His brother-in-law, Gary also came along. Now, Gary was a very enthusiastic fisherman. The man brought along at least four or five tackle boxes, the smallest of which dwarfed Pap's, probably a dozen different rods, "each for its own purpose," and so much other gear that I could not then process, nor can I recall now. It was a LOT. He had to rent a trailer to carry it in. There were a few other menfolk there, but I was six. I don't remember. Pap and Uncle Gary were the only ones that figure in my memory, or enough to stick anyway.

So. Little city boy me, off on his first camping and fishing adventure with my little suitcase and tackle box, piled into Pap's old Isuzu with

Grandma and a weekend's worth of food, the little pocket Jeep substitute pulling a Scotty travel trailer that was old and worn when my parents honeymooned in it, and we all set off to go meet the rest of the intrepid anglers at Snow Lake.

First off, I had never been in the woods before (that I can remember, at least). Second, I discovered (for the first time, not the last), that I do NOT like looking down a steep mountainside 8 inches from my door, on winding mountain switchbacks with no rails. Especially not when I know there is a trailer behind us, and I could easily imagine it falling down the hill and taking us with it. Third, I discovered I... well, let me tell you how the Snow Lake campground was at that time.

Imagine a primitive camp site. Not bad, no. Maintained. Clean. But no electricity. No lights. No plumbing. I was to discover THAT fact very quickly, to my dismay. All cooking done over gas. Pap had brought the Scotty trailer, but most everyone else was sleeping in tents on the ground, even Gary. His trailer WAS full of fishing gear, after all. At least Grandma was along to cook for us, because I was probably the second-best cook among the menfolk, after Pap. Who couldn't cook. And I was six. So.

Snow Lake is, or was (there have been a fire or three that have blown through since; it's a dry pine forest, and these things happen) quite beautiful. It's peaceful. Deer and elk amble through, there can be bear and bobcats and birds passing through your camp. Gentle breezes rustle the treetops, leaves chatter in the wind, and the slow lapping of small waves provides a counterpoint on the shore. Birds chirp, insects flutter, and the high mountain valley turned into manmade lake is the epitome of peacefulness.

I was terrified of the insects, though. You see, this was my first experience with the little bugs known as "horseflies" and "deer flies." I became convinced that every single insect was there for the sole purpose of painfully sucking my blood until I was a dry husk, and panicked every time one alighted on my skin. Yeah, city boy. I know. But I was six. A little slack would be appreciated, you know?

Pap, being a Country Boy from back when, was decidedly not impressed by my fears, by the way. More than once, I was told to stop throwing a fit, and get back to fishing. My six-year-old self wouldn't listen, and continued to throw "a right strop" every time some unknown bug approached.

The toilets.

Be me at six. Be accustomed to flushing toilets, to the common American porcelain throne. Have absolutely no concept or idea that anyone ever did their business anywhere else or in any other manner throughout history (other than babies pooping their pants, of course). Know with absolute certitude that no one ever went to the bathroom anywhere else, once they had achieved control over their bowels.

Now be introduced to the concept of an outhouse built over a giant hole in the ground. There are "leavings" of last week's campers and anglers in it. Once that hole is full, it will be covered over and the outhouse moved over a new hole in the ground. And a small enough person can fall in. Oh, and introduce the newly discovered fear of falling, thanks to the precipices over the edges of the road in. I became a big fan of making water while standing, and I held the rest the entire weekend. I was sorely uncomfortable; I'll tell you that much! By the end of the weekend, I was waddling.

But the fishing.

Pap, not trusting me to successfully avoid piercing my fingers in new and interesting ways (nor to get the knots in the line right), "volunteered" to maintain my tackle for me. Which was just fine by me. I had no clue what I was doing, anyway. So he attached a bobber, bit a couple lead sinkers to crimp them to the line about two feet below, tied on a hook, and pulled out a Can of Worms, Garden Variety, Mark One. He carefully showed me what he was doing as he threaded a squirming worm onto the hook, with a promise that next trip, I could do it myself. He made the first cast, showed me how to do it, then handed me the rod and reel, left me to do my thing, and went up the shore a little ways to go get his own line set.

Uncle Gary, meanwhile, had brought his trailer down to the shoreline. He spent (what seemed to me) ages and hours poring over which rod to use, what line, which bait, and so on and so forth. Having selected the appropriate gear, and spent another age putting it together, he stood up next to the water and started whipping that rod back and forth over his head, playing out more and more line with every pass, until finally with effort he flicked the rod one last time and his lure went sailing much farther out into the water than I believed possible. Immediately, he started slowly reeling it back in. He was going for the deep water, because it was the middle of summer, trout were cold water fish, and we were making so much ruckus on the short that nothing was going to bite there anyway.

Pap had by this point finished setting up his own pole, baiting his hook (Can of Worms, Mark One), and had cast his own more traditional line into the water, a scant three times as far from the shore as mine was.

My bobber, well, bobbed.

Pap (who was paying equal parts attention to his line, mine, and Gary's antics while I was absorbed in watching the show) immediately noticed, and hollered at me to give my pole a quick jerk to set the hook. So, I did. And Uncle Gary, with his untold expenses of fishing gear, watched as a six-year-old boy reeled in the first fish of the day, from a distance maybe twenty feet out into the water.

Pap baited my hook again. And about half an hour later, my bobber bobbed again. Another fish. Then Pap's bobbed. Then mine again.

Over the next several hours, Uncle Gary watched in growing disbelief as an old man and a little boy proceeded to absolutely skunk his high dollar setup by reeling in fish after fish, while he caught nothing at all besides floating sticks and lakeweed. To make matters worse, that little boy with the cheapest pole you could buy at Walmart and a can of garden worms not only caught the first fish that day, but the most fish, and the largest fish, all fine rainbow trout that were eaten with gusto that evening. Aside from myself, Pap was the only other person who caught anything at all that day, or the next (although to be fair, by that point he was assisting me with landing trout after trout instead of tending to his own line, so he probably missed more than a few from inattention).

Gary went home with his expensive tackle, his trailer, and empty hands. Pap drove us home on Sunday with a story he would proudly tell for decades thereafter, about how his six-year-old grandson skunked everyone, including him. And I?

I went home with my arms covered in painful and itchy bug bites, constipation, and a cheap fishing pole.

It was one of the best and most formative individual times of my childhood, and I couldn't wait for the next trip, although the next year would introduce me to my absolute all-time favorite fishing spot in the world, Indian Creek in Costilla County, Colorado.

But that place is another kettle of fish, as they say.

❧ 15 ☙

Tale of the Tame Deer

Told by Ella Haring Vanderburg (1913-2011)
Note by La Vaughn Kemnow Vanderburg: I present it as Mom told it to me. It was published in the 2010 Siuslaw Pioneer, a publishment of the Siuslaw Pioneer Association in Florence, Oregon, titled "As I Remember." I wrote the booklet; it is entirely about Mom's family.

I WENT TO SCHOOL IN A ONE-ROOM SCHOOLHOUSE AT THE PORTAGE on the North Fork of the Siuslaw River. I had to walk to school. By that time a primitive dirt road had been roughed out from the Portage downriver to the mouth of the North Fork—easily passable in summer, a challenge in wet weather.

One winter day my little sister Ruth and I were walking home from school when we saw a deer in the road. It came running toward us, tossing its head. We were scared—the deer was between us and our house, and we were afraid to try to get past.

This wasn't a wild deer. We had seen it many times—it wore a collar with a bell around its neck. It was a pet deer that belonged to Sam and

Margaret Woosley, who lived just across the river from the schoolhouse, and across the road from the North Fork Grange Hall; Sam's mother lived with them.

The deer was a very small spotted fawn when they got it; its mother was dead, and they had a permit to keep it. It was a buck, and when it grew up it got mean. The Woosleys would take food to the deer in a metal pail. Whenever the deer saw a metal pail, it thought it should get fed. So when Grandmother Woosley took the pail to the garden to gather vegetables, the deer would jump up and strike her in the chest with its sharp hooves.

We carried our lunches to school in metal lard pails. The deer must have thought we had food for it in our lunch pails.

It was prancing around and blocking the road so we couldn't go to our house on the hill, so we ran toward the old barn on the riverbank. We thought that if we went through the fence, the deer couldn't get to us. We knew how the deer had hurt Grandma Woosley, and we were afraid of it. But we didn't know the deer could jump over the fence!

When we got through the fence, we ran as fast as we could, screaming, "Help! Help! Help!" at the top of our lungs, as the young buck sailed over the fence and ran after us. A couple of times I picked up a stick to defend us against the deer, but each time the stick broke because it was rotten.

The faster we ran, the faster the deer ran. We were terrified.

When we reached the barn, we ran inside and quickly shut the barn door, leaving the deer prancing outside. We ran out the other end of the barn, still screaming.

Meanwhile, at our house on the hill, our father had taken off his shoes and was sound asleep on the floor in front of the fireplace. He had worked hard all day on the farm, and had been up all of the night before.

A man had robbed the bank in Florence, and at that time the only road out of the area was up the North Fork and over the Mapleton Hill. They had a blockade at the covered bridge by the Grange Hall. Our father, Albert Haring, and a couple of other armed men had stood watch at the bridge all night. Dad was so sound asleep he didn't hear us girls screaming.

But our mother heard us screaming, and woke Dad. Thinking maybe the bank robber was after us, he didn't even take time to put on his shoes, but grabbed his shotgun and ran the quarter mile across the soggy field in his stocking feet to the barnyard. And that was the end of the deer. We didn't eat the deer, but had to take it to the poor people in Florence.

The muck was a foot and a half deep in the barnyard, and Dad's socks were green, dank and smelly from the cow manure. I never knew whether Mom tried to get them clean or whether she threw them away.

16

Chasing the Wildlife

By Charles Scott

Finally, after what seemed like forever. It was the day. One morning in spring 1972 we rolled out on a trip that would take a month and 3400 miles. We would encounter the Blue Nile, dodgy infrastructure, snakes, and some of the most dangerous animals in Africa. It was an adventure right out of Boys Life.

As a child I couldn't understand but I now realize Daddy must have impaired his career as an Air Force officer. He searched out assignments based on family comfort and interest rather than with an eye to promotion. At that time the Air Force did not send Second Lieutenants to Viet Nam. They waited for you to be promoted first. My father had made First Lieutenant not long before but was either lucky or crafty enough to be sent to school which ended with him assigned as a postal officer in Kagnew Station, Asmara, Ethiopia.

In those days if you were military and ambitious there were three places outside the US you were likely to go: SE Asia/Vietnam to fight the Communists; Germany -to be a speed bump for communists; and Korea

-waiting to fight the communists again. While Ethiopia had its share of communists it was mostly a resting place for burned out spooks, and spook nerds (nerd spooks?), plus some actual military types to keep the lights on. None of these groups necessarily liked each other. The factions were: spooks, military, diplomats, and a few non-military support folks. Now, most of the military had a dim view of the spooks, the medical folks saw themselves a little separate from both groups were more closely connected to the Military since they were actually in the military. The same applied to the diplomatic crowd who were more aligned on the spook side of things and disdainful of the military. They were all unified in the feeling that SE Asia was definitely not somewhere to be.

The vagaries of assignment rotations and the requirements for personnel in SE Asia created some strange incentives for the military especially career military. Most people don't realize that the Viet Nam war wasn't exactly popular in the military either. There was considerable time and effort given to managing one's career to minimize the likelihood of being sent to the jungle. My father for example, had orders there once for sure. Which he managed to avoid by being selected for college and a commission. Because of this, some chose to come directly from the jungle to Africa since two back-to-back overseas tours would guarantee a longer time stateside before an overseas rotation became mandatory. Others took assignments in places that were less desirable. That's relative thing if the other option was a war zone.

David and I were born at just the right time to be American boys. In the most important years of our lives; from ages seven to eleven, we were fortunate to live in the America of our aspirations, the America that never really existed except in imagination and on family sitcoms of the day. US power was at its apex and the world had recovered from the Second World War. Two years earlier we all witnessed the miracle of Neil Armstrong walking on the moon. The world looked forward to a golden age if only we could get over this unpleasantness with the Soviet Union.

In Africa, Australia, Japan, or any number of tiny outposts, GI's and their families recreated the very best parts of home. It wasn't the America as it should have been, it was the America we believed it could be. But you can't imagine just how deeply weird it could be unless you lived it. Almost every family had one or more servants, and were wealthy in comparison to the local population, and the base was tiny chunk of America. A tiny chunk with gun towers along the wall and a machine gun nest at the front gate. A tiny chunk that had the necessity to move in convoy down to the recreation center on the Red Sea because banditry on the road made traveling alone dangerous. This contrasted with the poverty and undeveloped nature of the country. These things served to emphasize the sheer distance from everything we knew and understood.

To create a sense of normalcy communities had different rituals. There were the social rounds and occasions like a Dining In with the tuxedos and long dresses, ladies bridge afternoons and all that which for the most part had ceased to exist in the post war years stateside. There were regular fairs and celebrations for every conceivable holiday including the major ones like the Army-Navy Game, fireworks on the Fourth of July and the Junior Olympics. I remember we had cakewalks, the dunking booth with some unit CO or senior NCO trying to look like a good sport, the camel rides and little league games. It was all very small-town America. For entertainment we had the post movie theater with Saturday matinees for the kids, Armed Forces Radio and Television, USO shows occasionally, and organized trips for shopping, tourism, and hunting or fishing. The formal events could be very formal but if they weren't there was live music performed by local musicians. I've seen a lot of this type entertainment over the years a lot is mediocre at best but there can be amazing moments. Every place is a little different though and in Kagnew my mom told me the sound of that time and place was Creedence Clearwater. The local entertainers only knew a small number of American songs and really liked CCR. They would play the same few songs over and over.

We were almost completely isolated -letters taking weeks and packages taking months. News arrived late in the form of the International Tribune or weeks late home town papers and most often via Stars and Stripes newspapers. The fastest method was Armed Forces Radio and Television Service broadcasts. Getting ready for the holidays we eagerly anticipated the Sears Wish Book which arrived in August and the orders went out in September for delivery by Christmas -usually. But the Christmas trees would be flown in from Germany and Turkeys brought for Thanksgiving no matter what. Well, unless WW3 had kicked off and the Russkis were storming through the Fulda Gap then there might be a delay.

On the first and second safaris, once we left Asmara; with the exception of the two embassies on our route, there would be no way to communicate back with my mother faster than we ourselves could travel. It was a return to a pre-modern way of communication and we were completely on our own.

When we first arrived in Asmara there wasn't any base housing available. Instead, we rented a house in town. It was a two-story house surrounded by a tall iron fence in the front and a broken glass topped wall in the back. The landlord lived in an adjacent house immediately behind ours.

Like many Americans, my parents employed two servants. This was partly by necessity since they had the local knowledge to get many tasks down in and around the base and largely because it was comparatively inexpensive. There was also a feeling that this was a way to help the local people by giving them gainful employment.

The first, a Night Guard was a necessity because of the possibility of burglary by criminals known as shifties. There was even a little building on the compound for the purpose of housing the guard. Teclai was our Night Guard and house boy (Sorry 21st century that's the term of the day. Toughen up.). The original night guard was fired when found to be taking Daddy's bike out at night carousing. This was discovered one morning when he was riding to work. The pedals that worked great the day before somehow were welded solid to the crank the next morning. That night guard soon found himself seeking other employment. In his place came Teclai. He was living in the train station when somehow our landlord found him. Teclai was living there, having come to Asmara for school from an outlying town. He was interviewed and quickly hired. My parents set him up in the little night guard house with a bed, some shelves for books, and a little refrigerator. In many ways he was not a servant but a foster son and brother. A few months later when we on base there was no need for his services; but somehow, my parents found excuses to keep him on until he finally left us in Greece a few years later.

The maid was more of a luxury. Her name was Lhari. She was a woman of middle years who as the maid was Mistress of all things inside.

She took care of my little sister Kristin and; once he was born, my brother William. Lhari guarded her responsibilities fiercely and would belabor Teclai if she thought he was intruding into her domain.

Daddy had really gotten into the whole African adventure thing before we had been in Ethiopia long at all. He brought home a succession of creatures, curios, and trinkets. There was an antelope about the size of a small dog called a Dik Dik , a juvenile Baboon, swords real and wooden, and more. He was a soft touch and, in the market, it was almost guaranteed some young kid would offload whatever he had on my father.

Sometime after Christmas 1971 we moved on base. Shortly thereafter the Willys Overland Station Wagon appeared. In my imagination the conversation went something like this:

"Hey boys, Judy come take a look." Daddy said.

We would all dutifully troop out to the kitchen landing.

"Wow, cool, neato," we boys would say and go swarming down to the parking area with Kristin toddling along behind us.

"Just like Daktari!" we'd both say.

"Richard, what on earth is this behemoth. I certainly can't drive that." My somewhat more practical Mother would say. (I note here for the doubters, that she did not arrive in Africa any more accidentally than the rest of us. Which is to say, not at all.)

"It's for the safari," Daddy would swiftly explain.

"What safari?" Mother would ask.

"The safari we're going on after the little rainy season of course." Daddy would say. And that would be that.

This happened a lot, one day my father would come home and announce that we were going to Mazatlan, Bulgaria, Australia, or wherever. Any discussion with or objections from my mother were off stage but generally weren't much except in terms of ensuring adequate shelter (tent usually) and victuals (essential for three soon to be four kids) were available. And off we'd go.

Most of the lines drawn were in relation to living beasts. The baboon was a question of him or me. Mother being the better cook and so far, less prone biting the kids won out and no further small animals made an appearance. Except for the other Dik Dik arriving as tiny hooves sticking out of a grocery bag. That didn't fly either and was the end of

Daddy's abortive hunting career. His heart wasn't really in it. On the first safari one requirement was Daddy must bring Teclai along. By himself he wouldn't be able to supervise us and do all the other things needed to keep the expedition moving safely. Teclai was mandatory as a second set of adult eyes, strength, and most importantly local knowledge.

So, there we were. David and I all goggle eyed at the amazing Willy's Overland Station Wagon. It was huge, it was green, it was the ur-SUV. Equipped with a 6-cylinder motor and old school 4WD that involved getting out and locking the hubs on the wheels. Two doors, a split rear seat, and monster roof rack -later it would hold a packing crate big enough for two boys and a lot of gear. A safari was happening and we were going.

The first and most basic decision to be made was when to leave on the safari. Laying aside work obligations which were never discussed with us children, the most important consideration was the timing of the two rainy seasons. The rains would make roads very difficult and possibly impassable. The little rainy season ran into late March and early April and the big rainy season started in June. Additionally, the fact my mother was pregnant and due around July. That she would come was out of the question, but we couldn't be gone when she was likely to go into labor either. That left a narrow window of opportunity in late April to early June. Shortly after Easter we would be leaving.

We spent the months after Christmas getting ready for the trip. Early on my father "procured" some military tires for the jeep. From somewhere else we got a giant packing crate that fit perfectly in the roof rack. Two wooden military footlockers and "surplus" mail bags to hold gear. The first thing we did to make it ready was remove left side rear passenger seat. That left a jump seat on the right rear and extra room for gear.

When geared up for the trip we had the cargo box up top with gasoline, Coleman stove/lanterns/fuel, a metal trash can, water jugs, jerry cans of gas, "surplus" mail sacks containing a miscellany of gear including tools, spare tire inner tubes, and a jack. Also, up there was the folding camp table, lawn chairs, and other items that weren't water sensitive. In the back were the two footlockers holding most of the canned and preserved food, and an ice chest for the limited number of chilled items we carried. The tent, sleeping bags, and cots were in there along with our clothes and personal gear including the all-important books. The whole mass pretty much filled up the back of the Jeep and was surprisingly comfortable to lay on and read. The utterly essential books included: Travel guides for East Africa, maps, nature books, Hardy Boys, Tarzan, comic books, a couple of anthologies of short stories my father would read us at night, and lord knows what else. At the time I was reading a lot of Encyclopedia Brown and Hardy Boys, David favored Tarzan, and we both enjoyed reading or re-reading every comic book we could get. We were amply supplied with reading material.

The center piece in my memory was the tent. It was a blue-green canvas tent with a striped top you could fit six people in comfortably, as long as they were closely related and mostly small. I can still see how it goes to together even now. David and I were charged with the siting and erection of that tent for many years after. It was our first taste of adult responsibility.

Other preparations continued. Food was bought, fuel usage figured and the map carefully studied. That year one of our presents was a Zenith Transoceanic radio and it went along as well. Somewhere in there we all got safari suits with the belted jacket just like in the movies. We were very impressed. Daddy also got one of those Aussie slouch hats with one brim pinned up. We both admired it but David ended up wearing it most of the time. Since we were taking weeks of time off from school, we even had school assignments to do. Spoiler alert: no assignments were completed.

We were always pretty self-sufficient kids. At Kagnew; a snow globe America, we were safe and everything was close. On base it was safe to wander freely and we did so, even in places we definitely shouldn't have gone. Our inclination to independence and ability figure things out only grew stronger in that environment. Handling the camp was our job and the first taste of adult responsibility. We loved it. In the first days of the safari David and I learned how site the tent and set up the camp properly. Nothing was too big to handle for a couple of boys even if we were on the small size for our age. Typically, Daddy and Teclai would get the tent out of the jeep. Early on Daddy would site the tent and then David and I would spend the next thirty or so minutes fighting over the right way to set it up. I was always right. [Fact check: David says this is complete bollocks] After a few days we had mastered the task and my father rarely if ever intervened in camp set up again. We had already learned the basics having used the tent on trips down to Massawa including one memorable night camping on the beach. On the safari we eventually handled almost all the camp chores except for cooking. That was Teclai's job.

On this trip everyone was still learning though and there was a lot of experience to be had. One of the learning experiences were Vietnam Era C rations. That was a lot Ham and Lima beans. Well into my twenties I couldn't even smell Lima beans without gagging. For some reason though I still love Macaroni and Cheese. Teclai did the best he could with not very much and we learned a lot. David and I loved the little treats – M&Ms, crackers, and fruit cocktail. We were bemused by the toilet paper, coffee, and cigarettes. My Father either smoked the cigarettes or gave as gifts along the way. After a few weeks nobody regretted seeing the last of those rations.

After weeks of preparations, we were ready. Early one morning my mother got up. Fixed us a good breakfast and some sandwiches for lunch. Gave us all a big hug and kiss and stern injunctions to return with and not upon shields. We all once again trooped down to the jeep more hugs and kisses were disbursed and at last we were away. Headed south for the first major stop, Lake Tana source of the Blue Nile.

In the jeep we didn't have set places and alternated positions regularly but we all had preferred spots. My favorite spot was in the back cargo area laying on the soft gear in the mail sacks, it was a great place to read or nap. David liked the jump seat just behind the front passenger seat. Teclai was usually upfront but we all pretty much changed places throughout the day.

One early incident comes to mind from the first days of the expedition that demonstrates just how quickly things can get out of hand.

In the first two or three days out, we started having problems with the Willys. Stopping in a small village my father found a local mechanic to take a look at the truck. The mechanic found a problem with the distributor. Thinking for a minute he said, "I know of a place we can maybe get the part." Nearby out in the bush was a broken-down jeep from the war (or a war anyway) that still had a distributor cap. He and my father would go look there for any salvageable parts. So, my father left us with Teclai while he went with the mechanic to get the part.

WHILE MY FATHER WAS AWAY THE LOCAL VILLAGERS GATHERED OUT OF curiosity or boredom surrounding the truck. They were trying to get a closer look at the two little blonde headed boys -something they had probably never seen before. Teclai; being a teenager and all by himself, was overwhelmed. He was able to keep the crowd back. He leaned in the truck and told us to roll up the windows and lock the doors. David and I were afraid. The crowd of people was large enough and the most curious were trying to reach us that we climbed out of the windows and up on the roof rack of the jeep. We were well treed.

Fortunately; wherever my father had got to wasn't far and he arrived before we were on the roof long. He rolled up and just laid into the crowd shouting and using or threatening to use his fists forcing them back. Afterward, he helped us down and back safely in the jeep. He paid the mechanic, thanked the embarrassed looking village chief and we were back on the road.

Not long after we were camped for the night. By this point my dad's much admired Aussie hat had become David's property by right of conquest. It was many sizes too large and held on only by the chin strap and luck. He really loved it and rarely took it off. That night the chin-strap was hanging loose as it usually did. David and I were chasing each other around the camp fooling around the way boys that age do. Suddenly he was leaping around shrieking, "Snake, snake, there's a snake get it off get it off get it off!" Threw down the hat and ran away. We were all looking around for a snake. My dad Teclai both grabbed sticks and I had my BB gun at the ready. David was wigged out holding on to Daddy. We were all looking hard for that snake. The hat was poked, cautiously. We circled the camp. No snake. My dad turns, "David, where was the snake?"

"He was right there, next to my head," David said.

"Right where?" dad replied.

David indicated next to his right ear, "right here, daddy."

My dad picked up the hat. The chinstrap hanging snakily down. "I think you just saw the chinstrap, son."

David understood. He put the hat on and shook it. "That's it, that's the snake I saw."

The road to Addis Ababa from Asmara was a good one by African standards. Approaching the Blue Nile, it was a narrow and steep two lane blacktop with frequent hairpin turns. Sketching out a winding path down the side of a mountain it seemed every other turn was a structure that combined the worst parts of a hairpin turn and a bridge. As an engineering feat they were amazing, as a road it was terrifying. Just for extra fun factor the road was so narrow that when meeting oncoming traffic, it felt like our wheels were hanging in space. On every crossing the bridges shook and rumbled. His recent experience with a Fiat left Daddy little with faith in the quality and safety of Italian engineering. Especially, when far from auditors in the remote corners of the world. This transformed a difficult trip into a day of white-knuckle driving. Late that afternoon we finally reached the town of Bahir Dar on the shores of Lake Tana, source of the Blue Nile.

We found there a small town and a tiny hotel with an adjoining Italian restaurant. That night while Daddy recovered from the rigors of the highway with a desperately needed beer and we boys had a delicious spaghetti dinner. The rooms were spartan but clean and a welcome change after the preceding days of camping.

A day maybe two south of Lake Tana we stopped by the side of the river and set up camp nearby. Elephant droppings are huge, about the size of a kick ball and there were large amounts of them in the area. Teclai started kicking them around like a soccer ball. Soon, David and I played joined in on an impromptu game of soccer. They could be heavy and dense or light and fragile. Kicked too hard they had a tendency to disintegrate. Fragile as they were we soon ran out of the crappy balls. After the soccer and getting set up it was getting pretty late in the day.

All day we had been seeing some sort of partridge or quail like birds. As a consequence, my dad and Teclai had been talking about hunting birds and how tasty they were. Now my dad was never much of a hunter before and never would be in the future; but it seemed plausible enough that we could get a few birds. For hunting Daddy had his .22 caliber pistol -which as all the best hunters agree is the firearm most suitable for taking birds. That night before dinner it was decided that we would try to get some (note passive voice the international sign of bad decisions). David and I; the very models of youthful good sense, enthusiastically agreed and we all set about trying to find some tasty birds.

We made the dedicated effort to get a bird. Sticks were taken up and bushes were beaten, rocks thrown, possibly a round or two was discharged. A bird was not got. Fortunately, neither was anyone else. Mother would have been rather cross with Daddy if any of us failed to return all present and correct. It seems crazy now how just how unsafe the whole thing was but we were all young, and those were different times.

Eventually, we arrived in Addis Ababa. My father disappeared in to the embassy for a bit and used whatever phone connection was there to call mother in Asmara and check in. We spent a few days there buying additional supplies, fuel, and food. There were few larger towns until we reached the Kenyan border at Moyale so a top up was needed.

While very neatly drawn on the map; south of Addis the roads quickly went from paved to graveled and then to dirt. In many places they were mostly aspirational rather than actual. In the larger towns there was some paving but out past the last building the roads returned to dirt almost immediately. Once we were away from the paved roads of the north problems multiplied.

An immediate problem being almost no signage. For guidance we used the maps and compass my dad carried. He would take a bearing at crossroads and forks to keep us on track and occasionally otherwise to verify we were going the right general direction. But there weren't lot of roads to choose from and provided we stayed on a road we would get along pretty well. Daddy had made a board with the map wrapped around it and protected somehow from wear with the planned route marked on it. Studying the maps became a regular pastime and debate was a regular feature of our conversations. Whenever we stopped Daddy and Teclai would consult with the locals for any information on the roads ahead. A couple of times we gave rides to soldiers who helped us with directions to nearby towns. Plus, daddy had the compass.

Another larger problem was flat tires. Later my father would say that we had at least one flat for every day of the safari and sometimes two or more. Fifty-seven is the number I recall using the most -it was definitely a lot- but I don't think he ever really knew. He certainly wasn't one to let facts get in the way of a good exaggeration.

Because of this, we got NASCAR good at changing tires.

It worked like this:

Daddy would notice that the jeep had a flat so he would stop in the most level area he could find. No worries about traffic. There wasn't any.

David and I would climb up on the roof and hand down the patch kit and small tools -which eventually rode in the truck with us.

While Daddy and Teclai set up the jack David and I would get some rocks to block the tires. Then Teclai and my father jack up the jeep high enough to break the wheel nuts loose. David and I would then get the nuts off and stand ready to help with the breaking the bead -mostly running tools. Our major job was once the bead was off and started, we would go around the rim getting the tire off to access the tube. Then Dad or Teclai would fish out the tube passing it off to us. Our young eyes could pick out the holes fairly easily. Since water was short and pumping was hard, we preferred to visually identify any holes if possible. Once found the patch kit was put to good use on the hole and then we'd put the whole thing back together. After several days and a goodly number of patch jobs we had it all figured out. We could be back on the road in 30 minutes or so. It was in these exercises that we four bonded as a group and family. There were no children or adults just a team working together to solve a problem.

It took about a week but finally we arrived at the border. Moyale was a dusty little town with a lift gate and nothing else to block progress. It looked like something from an old movie right down to the little sentry box. Coming out the customs officer inspected the car and passed us through. At last, we were in Kenya. Mt Kenya, Amboseli, Tsavo, and the Serengeti plains called. Coming down out of Ethiopia the land had been gradually getting greener but passing into Kenya marked a change. In the hundred and fifty miles to Marsabit the climate changed quickly. As we pushed on the forests grew thicker and the roads improved.

South of Moyale the roads were once again pretty good two-lane black top. There were few or perhaps no fences and we saw large amounts of game. From the road we could see large herds of zebra and gazelle roaming freely, Giraffe browsing and everywhere were enormous termite mounds. The road wasn't built much over grade and we could easily turn off to stop and take a break or gawk at the wildlife.

After one fueling and leg stretch my father turned to us after we were back in the truck and pointing to the herd of zebra nearby said, "let's go see them closer."

Firing up the truck we wheeled over the plain closer to the zebra. As we approached, they spooked and bolted. Mistake. Daddy put the hammer down and started chasing them. David and I were holding on tight and howling in delight as the truck swayed and pitched. We were bouncing all over the rough ground dodging rocks and trees. Our good time got better once we failed to dodge one of the scrubby little trees and flattened it. That was even more fun. We were going bonkers. The next tree we hit by "accident" again and then a bunch more deliberately. Finally, Daddy decided we were pushing our luck in the tree department and slowed down easing up on the wildlife. We turned back to the Marsabit road.

After that modest delay Daddy had pushed hard to make Marsabit by midafternoon. Stopping at the ranger station to check in we all got out to look around and consult with the Park Rangers. The Rangers were friendly and as would be expected in a former English possession, spoke good English. The khaki uniforms with shorts and knee socks seemed exotic in comparison to what we were used to seeing at Kagnew. Ethiopia as the only nation in Africa not colonized by Europeans had many unbroken traditions so compared to the them the Kenyans seemed positively western. Dad spent a lot of time speaking with the Rangers for directions and learning about the park. We were warned of the elephants in the area including a rogue known as "One Tusk." One Tusk was an older bull elephant and thought to be potentially dangerous. We were warned to keep clear if we saw him. We were also warned about the other large animals especially the lions. The baboons were also a danger in that they would get in your vehicle if given a chance and tear it up looking for food. The plan was to camp the night and the next day tour the park. It would be our first close look at many of the animals that made Kenya famous. At least the ones too dangerous to chase.

Departing the station and we took a narrow dirt track to the volcanic lake that was our campsite for the night. It was heavily forested; trees and undergrowth looming over the road, with deep shadows even in afternoon. Occasionally; branches reached out slapping the jeep but the rest had learned their lesson, keeping just barely out of the way. When we stopped, the forest sounded a chorus of calls and bird song right out of every jungle adventure ever filmed. Several miles in, the road crested a ridge and we broke out into the green and gold bowl of the crater. Sapphire water made a perfect circle in the center of the crater. Not far away were villages and towns, but here was a tiny paradise that felt ancient and un-peopled.

Arriving late in the day, we drove around to find just the right place. With no formal campground we could choose anywhere that seemed right. Near the water mosquitoes would be fierce and there's only so much insect repellent will do. Not far from the road there was a clear area and we set up camp there. After camp was set, we walked down to the lake shore. In this tiny isolated wilderness, there was no road noise the skies were clear it could have been anytime in the last million years. My father had us just stand there, quiet and absorb it all. We lasted about 10 seconds. David and I spent a few minutes exploring and seeing the see-able. We joked that "Old One Tusk" (we had already granted him senior status) would be by shortly. As we left, over the lake, on the far shore, we saw movement in the trees. Movement that when watched carefully, seemed to be a couple of elephants. One may have had a single tusk.

We ate dinner and a little after dark David and I were off to bed. Just like every night my father and Teclai would stay up and discuss whatever it was big people talked about. Couldn't have been as interesting as GI Joes. Just like every night Daivd and I were dead asleep moments after laying down.

Suddenly, the metal trash can was crashing waking us up. The noise stopped after a moment and I could hear my father and Teclai talking but too low to understand. This lasted a minute or two and then it was silent again. I got out of the cot to see what was going on but in the dark couldn't see anything.

Suddenly, Teclai unzipped the tent.

"Quickly, get up and dressed," he said.

"Why?" I said.

He came in and started gathering our clothes and handing them to us. "Your Father said to get in the truck. You need to go, move."

As we came out of the tent Daddy gestured to the truck and said, "Get in the back, hurry."

David jumped into the back of the truck and I was right behind. Daddy slammed the rear doors and sprinted to the front taking the wheel. Teclai was in the front passenger seat.

To remind you, when traveling there were no set places and we all moved around. But we did have our favorite spots. Mine was in the back cargo area laying on top of the soft gear packed away in some mail sacks - it was a great place to read or nap. David liked the front passenger seat. Teclai took the jump seat. That night Teclai was up front. David and I were in the back cargo area.

The old Willys roared as it fired up and the dark night got less so in the headlights. Daddy jammed it into gear and pulled away from the campsite. Behind us we could see two elephants silhouetted in the light of a Coleman lantern. They didn't look happy. We all heard them trumpet. It was the announcement of deep trouble. One Tusk brought a friend. Daddy hit the gas. Hard.

The old truck's steering wheel juddered in Daddy's hand and the vehicle was slewing all over the dirt road. Every caution was left with One Tusk. We flew over the ruts and potholes that we so cautiously picked our way through a few hours earlier.

We made that turn to the Park Road on two wheels. The trees closed in blocking the moon's light. It was pitch black.

At that age you really don't understand anything but the most concrete dangers except as communicated by the behavior of those around you. Teclai and Daddy were both scared so we were too. In the back of the truck David and I were leaping around in agitation peering out the rear window.

Once we were on the Park Road Daddy had slowed down a little and we all relaxed just a smidgen. David and I peered into the darkness directly behind the old Willys. Then, in the glow of the tail lights. We saw the enraged visage of one -then two elephants. It was One Tusk and his plus one. The abstract became rather more...concrete. We were both jumping up and down in fear shouting "Daddy, Daddy they're right behind us, they're right behind us."

Daddy downshifted somehow finding more horses to most definitively run away. When David and I were all sorted out from being thrown around by the acceleration. I looked ahead. Directly in front of us was a sea of eyes.

Daddy slammed the brakes on forcing both the truck and two boys to a sudden stop. When I looked up, we were stopped with a river of Cape Buffalo running across the road just a few feet in front of us. They poured over the road for an eternal minute or two. All of which we spent looking before and behind wondering if it was going to be the most dangerous animal in Africa or only the third most dangerous animal that would smear us all over Kenya. After a moment of forever, the Cape Buffalo cleared away and we were able to move on. Looking behind the we saw no sign of One Tusk. At some point the elephants had lost interest leaving us the use of everything we valued.

Wanting to avoid any further Wild Kingdom moments we crept down to the village of Marsabit and parked spending the rest of the night asleep in the truck.

The next morning having slept comfortably in the back David and I showed no ill effects. Daddy and Teclai were both moving a bit slower. After stretching a bit daddy decided on a cautious return to salvage whatever the elephants hadn't destroyed. Our African adventure was over. Ended in near disaster.

Heading back to the camp. The road seemed a lot shorter, the way it does when you've learned a route so well you don't think about it anymore. Soon, we were pulling out of the forest into the meadow surrounding the lake.

It was a clear sunny day. We all cried out in amazement. Daddy said, "Damn, I didn't expect to find anything but a mud hole."

The elephants had left the campsite unmolested and our adventure would continue. For another thirty five years.

Dedicated with greatest affection to my brother David; Teclai who helped us so much; and my Father and Mother who made it all possible.

Marsabit National Park in Kenya is a beautiful place. Verdant forests, quiet roads and a volcanic crater lake. We were camped by the side of that lake in a vast meadow of elephant grass. It wasn't a designated campsite and there was no one else encamped nearby. We were a tiny spot of humanity in the night. Daddy was 32, my brother and I were 7 and 8 respectively and Teclai our houseboy (and semi adopted son) was around 18, maybe less. It was spring 1972 and we had been Africa less than a year.

⚜ 17 ⚜

Hunters Hunted

By David Hause

In the spring of 1968 I was about 15 months into my time in Vietnam (normal was 12 months but I had extended six months for an intra-theater transfer) and about nine months into of my time with what 5th Special Forces Group called a (maybe the) Special Operations Augmentation which supported something called MACVSOG (Military Assistance Command Vietnam Studies and Observations Group) which did the operations into Cambodia, Laos, and North Vietnam where the U.S. Government denied we had troops. Specifically, I was assigned to FOB 2 (Forward Operations Base 2, in Kontum, in the Central Highlands.

My team, ST Wyoming, was what was called a Spike Team, and was supposed to have twelve men (as opposed to a Recon Team, which had six) comprised of three Americans (team leader, assistant, and radio operator) and nine "indigenous" members, typically Montagnard tribesmen, one of whom was an interpreter (sort of.) Ours were mixed Jarai and Rhade tribe and one Sedang. The other two Americans were gone

(one injured in the U.S. on leave in January, one wounded and subsequently medically retired).

Anyway, we were in south-eastern Laos, which was the NVA (PAVN) area to rest, supply, or stage attacks into the Central Highlands. We weren't intended to fight these units but to locate for air assets to attack them. We were headed down a hill in thick forest, mid-afternoon, when we walked into a company-sized camp as the owners were entering from the down-hill side. Standard procedure was to break contact (the members emptied their weapons at the enemy and peeled back, reversing direction of travel in the original order) and call for extraction and attack air. We had recently passed over a bald hilltop which would be a good spot for helicopters to extract us and headed back that way. We seemed to have broken contact enroute to there.

We called. "Sorry, no extraction available, we'll try to get you in the morning." We spent an anxious but uneventful night. In the morning, we waited for extraction, all staying as low as possible behind fallen logs. Our turn continued as the hunted side. We did have a replacement for the missing radio operator, a new-in-country/first mission second lieutenant (the most junior of officers.) He left the radio and was crawling around the team, leaving the radio instead of monitoring it, trying to ensure that the experienced team members knew what they were doing, although he didn't.

During this wait, we got confirmation that we were now the hunted party as NVA soldiers started out of the woods exactly where we had the night before. When several had come out and part way up the hill, we sat up from behind logs and started the fire-fight. And reported to the extraction crew, who were inserting another team in the same general area, that we were having a fire-fight on our intended landing zone. "Hold on, we'll get to you." During the wait, we continued to get fire from around the base of the hill on the side we came out and farther around from there.

The first part of the extraction crew arrived overhead, the fire support portion, two Air Force A1-E Skyraiders. (This was a Korean War hold-over, propellor driven, slow-flying (compared to the jets), carrying large amounts of bombs, rockets, and .50 caliber machineguns.) But best, they had radio compatibility so we could talk to them and they were slow enough to see us on the ground, neither of which was true with the jets. Suddenly, our side were the hunters again.

I reported where we getting the most fire from and, politely, the lead pilot, using our radio frequency to talk to his wingman, said "This is Hobo 34, I've got the friendlies in sight and I'm rolling in hot." And he went into a dive and dropped napalm on the tree line I had indicated. No more fire came from there and the rest of the day was uneventful.

EIGHT YEARS AFTER I CAME HOME FROM VIETNAM, I STARTED MEDICAL school because I wanted to be a forensic pathologist. The Army Health Professions Scholarship program paid for the last three years, in exchange for a service obligation. By the end of that obligation, I knew I was where I belonged, stayed, and retired after a bit over 36 years.

❧ 18 ❧

One of those days...

By Denton Salle

The sun was still high enough that the lengthening shadows weren't tempting the wildlife, so I figured I had an hour or so to wait yet. The day was warm in the West Texas sun, but the temperature would drop a bit after dark. The breeze coming up to the deer blind pulled the scent of sage with it as it rustled the leaves of mesquite trees that surrounded us. Down the game trail I was watching, I could hear ducks and geese in the stock tank, as the locals called the artificial pond we dug to supply both the cattle and the wildlife. Well, had dug. Dang contractor won't let me play with the digger.

Despite our plans, we got more hogs than anything else sadly.

But there were enough deer and turkey on the property since we hog-fenced the feeders. No sense wasting deer feed on monsters that will eat anything, including each other. The deer feeder by the tank was fenced and we didn't hunt over it. We wanted Bambi to have a safe spot. Hogs

now...we wanted them to just die. Dang things were incredibly destructive and horridly fertile.

I clambered out of the blind. These dang knees just needed replacement bad but honestly, who has time for two six-week recovery periods?
Especially when Vitamin I works. Actually, better than a lot of those
fancy drugs. The joints do kinda makes one wish for the old days when
the local drugstore sold opiates. I stretched and I decided I need to,
ahem, how to put this. Talk to the nature spirits. Return my coffee.
Water a tree. You get the idea.

I paused a moment to listen to the call of a hunting hawk. Lord it
was a beautiful day. Idyllic is the fancy word, though the locals say "God's
Country." Except for those stupid windmills on the horizon.

"Bird choppers" as my neighbor down the road calls them. If they
enforced the laws on killing birds of prey fairly, the fines would put them
out of business and then maybe we could get a nice nuclear plant instead.
But I ain't fool enough to think anything's fair in this life. Not when a big
company can buy itself a congress critter.

The boys and I had been hunting for three days now. One more to
go. The four days following Thanksgiving were always hunting or fishing
trips for us. Mostly because Grandma came to visit. Now don't get me
wrong. I love my mother-in-law. She's good people. It's just she and the
missus snipe at each other constantly.

I don't get it. The missus and my momma get along like best friends,
but her own mother... well, we go hunting. To escape being collateral
damage.

The boys had each taken a nice buck by now, and I hadn't. I was
trying for fun to hunt with a single action long colt, because why not? It's
not like Texas deer are large. But it did mean I needed to get closer than
normal and I long ago had realized I wasn't that good at stalking. Sitting
still for hours waiting, that I could do. Sneak up on Bambi...not so much.

Anyway, the boys had been giving me crap of it for the lack of a kill.
The oldest was threatening to start telling people his dad's Indian name
was "Vegetarian" which he claimed was Comanche for "can't hunt." The
other made me a salad for lunch.

I was mostly content to let them tease. Never told them how many
times I didn't even load the rifle when they were younger. After all, we

work on the "you shoot it, you clean it" rule. So, getting skunked wasn't all bad. Especially when they were littler and you clean it translated into you clean it with Dad's help.

Anyway, it was the evening of the third day, and I had been watching the game trail that led to the waterhole on the property. Dang thing was a nightmare to get to hold water in this sandy soil. Finally had to line it with clay. Finally, as I said, my bladder was sending me a message. So, I walked back a bit away from where I was watching and found a tree that was in need of water. Heck, this is West Texas. They all need water. This one was big enough to give me a little cover, while I watered it. Nice brush on either side of I didn't flash the cattle. Wouldn't want to scare them, you know.

I was taking care of business when I hear a noise that sounded just like a cow chewing its cud. Close-up. I looked over, moving slowly. We leased the land for cattle and I knew several of the cows had calves. Those walking meatloaves will stomp you if they think you're messing with the calves.

Nope. It was a deer. A doe. Couple years old I'd guess. Standing there staring at me.

Boy later said it was probably thinking "that's all he's got?"

I swear I should have sold him when he was still little and cute. That ship is long sailed.

I drew my .45 Navy Colt Conversion repro slowly from it's calvary holster. Moving slow. Raised the gun and aligned the sights. The silly thing kept looking at me. I considered it as it considered me. Finally decided it should know better.

I shot it. One shot. Dropped right in place.

I waited a few minutes, holding dead still. Always a good idea. Know people who lost animals. Know one guy who got ribs broken when a deer kicked him. So, I stood there, all the time hoping I won't get bit by something someplace not normally exposed. I just, ahem, tucked myself in when the boys pulled up on the mule.

"You got one, Dad?" the younger exclaimed. "With that relic?"

Before I could reply, his older brother asked, "Dad, why is your fly open?"

Well, She's Not Wrong

By Alan Andrews

Before I was born, my parents were on a deer hunt in Colorado. Mama wasn't really a serious huntress, but she enjoyed the outdoors.

Daddy left her in a blind one morning, and moved on to another location.

When he came to get her later in the morning, she was very excited, and told him, in great detail, about a mountain lion that she'd seen in plain view for quite a while: maybe 15 minutes or more. She said it never seemed to be aware of her presence, and she never felt in danger.

"Why didn't you shoot it?" Daddy asked.

Mama immediately replied, "but you told me not to shoot anything but a buck!"

❧ 20 ❧

Rupert

By JL Curtis

We've been hunting down in central Texas for quite a few years now, and since it's managed land, there are restrictions.

One of those restrictions is no yearling deer.

Enter Rupert...

The first time we saw him, he was a yearling 4 pointer, but he was a 'tad' strange. As in he was running around with yearling does, and a few fawns. This is not normal behavior for a young buck.

I saw him three or four times during that year's hunt, always with the yearling does. Couldn't shoot him or the does, so they just killed any chances at a decent deer.

Well, other than the one that walked up on me while I was taking a leak. You ever try to finish your business, slip your pistol out, and not startle the deer?

Suffice to say, that didn't end well. By the time I got my pistol out, range was about ten feet, the doe looked at me, flipped her ears, and bounded over the fence. Which, by the way, put her in an area that I couldn't shoot toward.

So, I go back to my stand, cussing myself, and here comes Rupert and his harem again. Zilch for the next two days other than Rupert and his harem. One of the other hunters was ensconced in his blind that evening and hadn't seen much either. Finally, a couple of yearling does came over where he was and he looked them over, then saw something behind them. The harder he looked the more it looked like a deer, but it was also getting dark, so he wasn't sure. The yearling does started moving back the way they came and he pulled his rifle down, only to have that 'possible deer' move in among the does. You guessed it. Rupert!

The next year, we go back, and Rupert is now no longer a yearling. He's gonna be dinner! Except he showed up with the new crop of yearlings bouncing around him. And he always kept some of them between him and the blind. Dammit! Saw him twice, a couple of others saw him but couldn't get a shot either. Skunked us again.

Third year, and everybody is after Rupert. Note- He's now survived multiple hunters for an entire year, and is apparently one of the group of deer that come to the house in the evenings to get fed by the wife of the owner because she likes to 'watch' the deer. And of course, we can't shoot them by the house.

Out and in the stand early the next morning, and I can hear deer moving in the underbrush. Metaphorically licking my chops, I ease the rifle out of the blind. And here they come. Yearling doe, yearling doe, yearling doe, Rupert (now a 6 pointer), surrounded by three more yearling does and two fawns. @#%#%(*&! I almost yelled at them to see if I could spook the yearlings and get a shot on Rupert, but I didn't. I waited patiently scoping Rupert and hoping for a clear shot. And hoping, suddenly Rupert is gone. Grrr...

That evening no deer, but Rupert was down by another stand doing the same thing! They didn't get a shot on him either!

That sumbitch made the rounds of all the blinds, always 'escorted' by his little herd of yearling does and occasionally fawns. Skunked us again.

A couple of months later, we went back for a second hunt. Asked about Rupert and the owner said he hadn't been taken, but a number of hunters noticed his behavior. All weekend I see a total of four deer. You guessed it. Rupert and three yearling does bouncing around him, again! And no shot, again! #@$%#*%#~!~~

The last round of hunting, I didn't see a single deer. Not even Rupert. But I'm sure that sucker is still out there, probably still playing with the yearling does, and using them as cover. This year, things are gonna be different... Rupert's going down! Maybe... I hope...

A Colorado Coon Hunt,
Or: Why You Shouldn't Do That

By Dawn Keenan

My father used to love to hunt, before life and physical pain got in the way. Way back before I was around (I'm 37 years old now, for reference) Dad would hunt with a friend of his, Lloyd.

One of the things they enjoyed hunting was raccoons. Now, this is not as common in Colorado as it is in southeastern states, because while we have raccoons in abundance, what we don't have are trees. As I understand it, since I've never actually hunted raccoons, the easiest way to hunt them is to get them up a tree with dogs, so that they stay in one spot long enough to be shot. Lacking trees tends to make this a much more difficult sport, but raccoons are also destructive and love to steal eggs from hen houses... along with cat food and any other edible that's left lying around.

Well, Lloyd had a pack of coon hounds that he had named after characters from the TV show Gunsmoke. He had Doc, Festus, and

Gunsmoke. When Dad got a blue tick female, he decided to continue the theme, and named her Miss Kitty.

Now, please imagine with me, a blue tick coon hound, which can weigh in up to 85 pounds, and has a baying "barooooooo" of a voice. My parents lived on the farm at this time, so of course Miss Kitty was free to wander around the property, and she was reportedly particularly good at coming when she was called.

My father, being the man he was, had trained his dog to recall to "here kitty kitty kitty!"

Of course, being the man he was, he took great amusement in stepping onto the porch and calling "Here kitty kitty kitty!" in front of people who had not yet met Miss Kitty. Around the shop or the house would come nearly 100 pounds of coon hound, "barooooooo"ing at the top of her lungs out of excitement.

Dad got entirely too much entertainment out of not warning people when he did that.

Anyway, after they got Miss Kitty trained and working with the rest of the pack, they went hunting. They'd been reasonably successful with three dogs, though obviously not perfect since it's called "hunting" and not "catching." Clearly, four dogs were going to be better than three, less chance of the raccoons slipping away.

I believe this story happened on their first full hunt with Miss Kitty, but I could be wrong.

The way Dad told it, it was a pretty slow night hunting coons, they hadn't had much luck and were nearly ready to head home, when the dogs picked up a scent. The only problem was they were in the middle of a field, headed to a tree line along a fence, as you see in southeast Colorado. The trees here are either lucky enough to be near a reasonably regular water source, of which there are approximately two, or are carefully cultivated and cosseted for shade for homes or livestock. Dad and Lloyd were in the middle of a plowed field at least a hundred yards from this tree line when the dogs started "barooo"ing ahead of them, so they started running towards the pack.

I never could get the same answer out of both of them about what went wrong. Dad said all the dogs must have just missed the scent until they were on the far side of the coon. Lloyd swears that Miss Kitty just didn't like him and did it on purpose, trying to get him. Whatever the actual answer, the dogs were chasing the coon into the plowed field, instead of the trees.

I should note for anyone who isn't familiar with raccoons, that the reason the easiest way to hunt them is to get them in a tree is because when under threat a raccoon will do anything it can to get some elevation. Their natural response is to climb.

This particular coon was no exception, and the first path to "up" the coon found was Dad. That coon scrambled up his legs, across his back and onto the top of his head and started hissing at the pack, who were all coming up fast from behind and "barooo"ing because, well, that was their job. The raccoon was definitely not satisfied at the level of safety provided by its current perch, but wasn't about to give it up at this late date to find something better.

Friends, have you ever seen an angry raccoon? They grow approximately 3 times in size, for the hair standing up. They have a mouth full of sharp, insect eating and scavenging teeth, and they have thumbs. Now we have twenty pounds of furious and terrified teeth and fur and thumbs, clinging to my dear father's head.

Dad was absolutely not pleased with the situation, all things considered. Lloyd was too busy laughing until he couldn't breathe to be much help, and the dogs were all happy as could be. Of course, they were, they were living the dream! They got to chase and tree and they got to be near one of their favorite people.

Dad eventually realized that he could either solve the problem himself or end up on the ground with an angry raccoon and a pack of dogs fighting on top of him. So, he pulled out his carry pistol, his rifle being rather awkward for the situation, and screwed the barrel up under the coon, right by his right ear, and pulled the trigger. The coon fell off his head, the dogs got it instead of Dad, and Dad was pretty much deaf from that day forward in his right ear.

Dad and Lloyd continued to tell the story as a cautionary tale about hunting raccoon without trees.

Kitty
Cedar

AFTERWORD

You know, you shouldn't shoot fish. It's faster to use dynamite.

I don't recall who first told me stories about dynamiting fish, and if I believed half the ones I was told, there was a lot of shenanigans going on back in the day. It wasn't about fact or fiction, though. It was the story-telling, and the laughter, and behind that, the hunting. I've been a subsistence hunter - we'd have been a very hungry family without caribou in the freezer, those Alaska winters. My tag wasn't the only tag in the family, and I certainly wasn't the primary hunter. But I knew full well what taking a 'bou meant to my ability to eat, and eat well.

I'm hoping that you found some memories, and thoughtful moments, along with the laughter in these stories. There will be more like them (but different!) in the second volume. Something you may have also noted is how generational hunting is. It's passed down from the elders to the small ones, who listen with big ears and bigger eyes to the hunting stories. Keep that in mind, when you read this, and perhaps when you pass on a copy to someone you'd like to give a reason to learn the ancient art of taking home food from the wild, the purest form of feeding one's family, and the greatest sport of them all: life. Can't live long if you can't eat.

Hunting these days is, some say, a relic of another time. You don't

have to hunt to eat. I say it's a way to be closer to your food and the essence of what it means than any supermarket can get you, that's for darn sure. It's not easy, and it's not supposed to be. It will teach you to respect the land, the animals, and perhaps even yourself.
—Cedar Sanderson

Some of the authors in this book have other books and stories you might enjoy:

JL Curtis - Showdown on the River
Lawdog - Ghosts of Malta
Kelly Grayson - Perspectives
William Lehman - Shadow War
Kat Stevens (as Kat Ainsworth) - Handgun Hunting
La Vaughn Kemnow - Alaska Bush Mother
LA Behm II - Hero's Lament
DL Campanile - Fire's Maiden
Peter Grant - Brings the Lightning
Clair Kiernan - Gone with the Zombies
Denton Salle - Sworn to the Light
Cedar Sanderson - The Ratel Saga (with Lawdog)